SOCIAL MEDIA NETWORKING

HOW TO USE SOCIAL MEDIA TO GET THE JOB
YOU WANT, FIND LOVE, GET BUSINESS
SUCCESS AND BOOST YOUR TRAVEL
EXPERIENCE

TIM LEWIS

Published by Stoneham Press Ltd
Copyright © 2018 Timothy Michael Lewis
Special thanks to Ann Lewis for editorial work.
First Edition
ISBN : 978-1-910802-07-6

To Rachel McFeely 1969-2011

BACKGROUND

INTRODUCTION

The world has changed from when I started work in the 1990s. Social media has transformed the way that people do business, conduct their relationships and has helped change the modern world.

Its ills are well-known and publicised. This book is about the positive side of social media. It is an exploration of how people have used social media to get ahead in their lives.

Before 2014 I had barely used social media. I had a LinkedIn account but I did not really use it for anything particularly social: my connections were a collection of recruitment agents and former work colleagues. My Facebook account was my way to keep in touch primarily with friends of my late wife, Rachel.

After leaving my corporate job in March 2014, I began writing and self-publishing several books (three time travel novellas and then later three fantasy books) and was faced with the great dilemma that many a new entrepreneur is faced with: I have a product, how do I sell it?

So I started researching marketing (mainly by listening to podcasts on the topic) and ended up stumbling across the concept of social media marketing. This is using social media to market products. This appealed to me as it was relatively low cost compared to many other marketing methods. One of the best sources of information on this was Social Media Examiner, who run the Social Media Marketing World conference in San Diego every year.

I became much more active on social media and tried, with varying degrees of success, a lot of automated and quick ways to try and use social media to sell books: regularly tweeting out book details, for example. But honestly these efforts weren't too successful.

Despite being a fiction author, I found myself becoming way more interested in social media than in my books. But still I couldn't crack the "selling books on social media" thing. I would like to say that this book was the "selling books on social media" book. But it isn't: I still haven't mastered that.

This book is based on the realisation that I had in 2017 that while I still haven't quite worked out how to sell anything on social media, I have made a great number of friends and connections. These connections have brought me quite a few pieces of work (notably for the Alliance of Independent Authors and Social Media Examiner) and also have hugely enriched my travel experiences.

I was originally going to write a book about my own thoughts on how powerful connections on social media are, but a chance conversation on an interview on my podcast with Clare Josa that got me thinking. I mentioned the book to her after the recorded part of the interview and she said "well if you want any case studies, then let me know."

It suddenly occurred to me that case studies would make the book so much better, as while I'd had opportunities from the connections I'd made, I knew that there were many people out there (including many people I knew) with much better rewards from their use of social media.

So in autumn 2017 I posted the following on my Facebook personal profile:

> *As some of you may know I am (slowly) attempting to plan out a Social Media book about how an individual can use Social Media to enhance their life. But ideally I'd like some more case studies. I'm looking for people with stories of the following:*
>
> *1) People who have managed to get a new job by making a connection on a social network at their dream company.*
>
> *2) Someone who has first met their romantic partner on Social Media (I'm kind of assuming they do actually get off it at some point for this).*
>
> *3) Any great opportunity that people have got via a connection that has developed on Social Media (e.g the chance to speak somewhere)*
>
> *4) Any times when you have gone to a new location and had fun by meeting contacts that you have only previously met on Social Media.*
>
> *I am looking for cases where Social Media was the first connection point, even though in most cases clearly the relationship may have developed elsewhere.*
>
> *I am NOT interested in people telling me about their social selling/online funnels/get rich quick social media course.*
>
> *Please comment here or DM me.*

In all honesty I was expecting maybe three or four replies. In total I had 40 responses. I had lots of replies from people with fantastic stories about how they fulfilled one or more of these categories. I was shocked and excited by this, and the focus of the book transferred from my meagre experiences and theoretical knowledge to creating a book based on the actual real life examples. So I went away and organised interviews with as many of the people as I could. Some dropped out, some we just couldn't get the appointments booked due to scheduling and some just weren't that relevant.

In total I ended up interviewing 20 people. Many of those people had amazing stories covering multiple of the categories above. There were also some great stories that didn't cover any of those categories above but I have included, as I think they represent more topics I just hadn't thought of when I wrote the post. To avoid the book ballooning to too large a size (and to make my tight book deadline) I've taken the best category story from each person and included it here. Some are full conversations and others are just the description of one of the categories above.

In terms of my editorial policy, I had the interviews transcribed, and I have tried to maintain as much of the original audio conversation as possible to maintain as much of the personality of the interviewee as possible.

In 2014 I knew none of people I interviewed: they are all people I've met either on social media or at conferences since then. I consider most of them as friends. One of the most basic advantages of social media is that you can expand your network of friends away from just your local area or your workplace. But this book isn't just about making friends on social media, its about the more tangible benefits that those connections can bring.

Before getting onto the interviews, I'm going to take you through a very short crash course in social media, to make the interviews make more sense to those of you who aren't used to the technology. After the interviews I'm going to round up what I've learned and summarise the steps you need to be taking if you are looking to utilise social media networking in your own life.

CRASH COURSE IN SOCIAL MEDIA

So firstly, what is social media? There is a surprising lack of clarity as to what the definition is if you search on Google for the answer. Many definitions start by defining it as web sites like Facebook, Twitter, Instagram, Pinterest, Snapchat and LinkedIn.

FOR OUR PURPOSES I am going to define it as any technology where people can find and connect with other people and have conversations with multiple people around a topic. I would not consider e-mail and solely messaging platforms like Whatsapp as social media, as they tend to be closed in terms of discovering new people to communicate with. I'm also not counting dating sites like Match.com as social media as they are mainly search-based in finding people to message. Though I admit it's a thin divide.

THERE'S ACTUALLY a large variation in how these platforms work. Some are primarily search based while others are primarily community based. Most have some element of one or the other. Some platforms are open, as in anyone can see what you post, like Twitter, and others like Facebook by default only show your posts to a select group of individuals, usually people you have selected as connections. Almost all platforms support some kind of private or group messaging function where you can individually and privately communicate with one or more people on the network.

MOST PLATFORMS LET you specify a set of people and companies to follow or friend. Sometimes this has to be a two way thing (for example normally Facebook friends have to follow each other) but in other cases, like on Twitter or for companies on Facebook, you follow something and it's up to them to determine whether they follow you back. Being a follower of someone usually gives priority to people seeing your posts and lets you privately message the person on the platform. It is also possible to specify that only people you are friends with can see your post on sites like Facebook.

WHEN I REFER to a post I am talking something you have created and uploaded to the social network. Depending on the platform, this might be a piece of text, an image, a video or a live video stream from a phone or computer, which is known as Live Video, which other people can interact with and comment on as it happens. Twitter supports this with a platform known as Periscope and Facebook supports it with a platform known as Facebook Live. So if people refer to a "Periscope" or "Scope" or "Facebook Live" or "Live" they are talking about either viewing or creating one of these kinds of live video posts.

THE SOCIAL MEDIA platforms work by showing you posts, depending on who you are connected to, on a main "newsfeed" or letting you search for posts from other people by keywords. In the early days of many of these networks, people added a # (or hash) sign to the front of words in the text of their posts to make it easier for people interested in a topic to find their post. So searching for #fishing on Twitter will find you lots of posts of pictures of people holding up fish. You can also search for "fishing" and get similar results now, but with the hashtag #fishing you know that people have explicitly added this to their posts. So it won't find any posts where people say "fishing for compliments" for example. Many platforms let you click on these hashtags to show you other posts also containing the same hashtag, to make navigation on the site easier.

IN GENERAL PLATFORMS will let you interact with posts by clicking buttons to show an emotional reaction such as "liking" a post or by leaving comments which are on many platforms like mini-posts attached to the main original post. So for example, I might post "Does anyone know of any good films?" and someone can leave a comment saying "I really like the film Casablanca". Some social media networks support threaded comments where people can reply to the comment on the post with their own comments, so someone could comment about Casablanca in the post above on the comment mentioning Casablanca.

WHEN YOU CREATE an account on these platforms you need to select a handle or name that appears next to your posts and is used to reference you on that platform. So on Twitter and Instagram I am "stonehampress" for example. Not all platforms require a unique name that no one else has chosen, but if you have a common name (like I do), then on some sites like Twitter you may need to give some thought as to what handle to create.

ATTACHED TO YOUR HANDLE, most platforms let you create a profile, where you can write a piece of text and attach a series of images describing yourself. On most platforms this is fairly limited, but on some platforms like LinkedIn these can be extremely long and varied. These profiles appear in searches if they contain words that people are searching for.

When someone else posts something that they consider to be related to you, they can include your handle in their post (this is sometimes called "tagging") making it more likely you will see the post in your main feed. This can be a great way to bring other people into a conversation. But if abused it can be very annoying.

ON MOST PLATFORMS when you aren't using the site, it will either send you notifications on your mobile phone when things happen, or it will build up a queue of notifications of things like being followed/friended by a new person, when a post mentions you, and comments and reactions to your posts. Depending on how much you use the platform you can receive notifications for posts and all sorts of other random events the platform wants to notify you about.

A MUCH TALKED about thing is "the algorithm" in social media. This refers to how each platform works out which posts to show you, and which posts will cause you to receive a notification. Once you have followed a large number of people there become a huge number of potential posts and notifications for you to see when you use a social media platform. The platform has some code which prioritises particular posts and notifications. When this code changes it causes a lot of consternation in social media marketing circles as it'll often ruin whatever method they were using to get their marketing posts in front of their customers.

ON SOME OF these platforms you can pay to advertise to ensure that people see your posts in their newsfeeds when they connect to the network. This is done even for some companies where someone has followed their Facebook page. Company page posts are right at the back of the queue for being shown to their followers. Typically only a very low percentage of followers of a Facebook page of a company will see any of their posts on their newsfeed. This percentage of people who see the posts is called "reach" and posts where an individual or company hasn't paid for extra reach is called "organic" traffic.

As all the social networks have filled up with more and more posts from people looking to receive attention for both business and pleasure, it has been progressively harder to use the old traditional broadcast style "buy my product" type of posts to sell products.

Let's look at the platforms in turn and see which features apply to each and mention any of the special features of each:

TWITTER

Twitter is a fantastic platform for finding relevant people. The platform is extremely public, in that everyone can see everything you post. When you log in, you see a feed of the posts of people who have followed.

Twitter have fairly recently introduced an algorithm which means that it reorders which tweets you see first based on your previous interactions with people on Twitter. Twitter supports famously short text message posts (up to 280 characters. This used to be 140 characters but has recently been increased), but you can also attach images, GIFs and videos to these posts (known as tweets).

You can tag other users by using their handle prefixed with the @ (at) symbol. If you want to interact with a tweet you can either like the tweet, retweet the tweet (which shares it with your followers) or you can reply with your own tweet. Generally speaking the best conversations are based on a series of tweets replying to each other.

THE PERISCOPE APP (which is a company Twitter took over) lets you live-stream video to Twitter. What this means is that on your Twitter client you will see a post containing a video like a live TV broadcast from wherever the person doing the broadcast is. This can be done from a phone, or with the right software from a desktop computer. You can respond to these broadcasts within the individual post (unlike normal Twitter where you can only respond with new tweets). When the broadcast is finished, you can replay the video and it turns into a tweet with a video replay attached, also including comments made while the broadcast was running.

TWITTER LETS you pick a group of users and allocate these to what is called a Twitter list. You can then view the tweets of people in these lists as if they were the only people you were following. As the tradition is to follow most people back who follow you, this gives you a great way to keep an eye on particular groups of people who would otherwise be lost in your main twitter feed.

ANOTHER TWITTER specific feature is what are called Twitter chats. These involve a group of people agreeing to all monitor and use a hashtag in a particular period of time. Typically this involves one person posting questions using the hashtag and other people answering those questions and talking to each other using tweets always including the hashtag. The free tools Tweetdeck and Tweetchat allow you to do these more easily. As an example, at the moment Social Media Examiner is running the #smechat Twitter chat.

TWITTER IS THE "CONFERENCE SOCIAL MEDIA" network, in that a Twitter hashtag for the conference and the Twitter handles of the speakers are usually prominently displayed at events.

Facebook

Facebook is the biggest social media network. It is also a very innovative company in terms of updating the network regularly with new features, making it often very hard to keep up with their latest changes. A Facebook post is either a piece of text of almost any length to which you can attach a number of images or photos.

You can also post GIFs, create events and create Facebook Live broadcasts, where you stream out live the contents of your phone, in a similar way Periscope does on Twitter; however on Facebook the experience feels much more built-in to the platform, and the people who can see the broadcast can be set to be more limited. You can comment on posts using text, images and videos in a very similar way to a main post. For all posts and comments you can "react" to the post using a series of emojis - like, love, haha, sad, wow and angry. This is a fairly new addition, but does allow expressing emotion on posts with a negative theme.

ON FACEBOOK, the basic profile is what is called a personal profile and you can send invites to people to connect with you as a friend. If they accept then you can see each other's posts by default. It is possible to set your posts to be seen by everyone (public) or a sub-group of your friends but the default is for your friends to be able to see your posts.

FOR COMPANIES and organisations Facebook gets you to set up a Facebook Page. People with profiles can like the page which means that these posts can be seen potentially in their newsfeeds. However the algorithm for determining which posts are seen favours friends over companies, and to ensure their followers see their posts companies need to pay. They can also push their posts onto people who aren't following them based on all sorts of criteria, which is the world of Facebook Advertising.

THERE IS ALSO the concept of Facebook groups: these are areas where only people who are members of the group can post and see posts in that group. These posts can also show up in your newsfeed and you can post and comment on them if you are a member of the group. There are huge numbers of Facebook groups on a whole range of topics that people have set up, and many of the stories in this book started because of connections made in Facebook groups.

A NEW FEATURE shared by both Facebook and Instagram is "stories": these are a series of images/videos that a user posts which only last 24 hours. This is almost a direct copy of Snapchat and helped push Snapchat's recent decline. The fact that they disappear encourages people to watch them to see what the person sharing the story has been doing.

LinkedIn

LinkedIn is the "professional" network. It started out mainly as a site which more or less was just electronic copies of people's resumes. This is why the profiles on LinkedIn are much longer and more formal than on the other platforms. It's a very strong platform for search. Like Facebook you invite someone to connect and they either accept or reject your connection.

IF THEY ACCEPT THEN the connection is two-way, each of you will see each other's posts. My experience is that people look at posts less often on LinkedIn than on Twitter and Facebook but people tend to search more for people on it. LinkedIn supports text, image and recently video posts. It also has a long-form text publishing platform that is available for anyone to see and discover.

On LinkedIn, as well as being able to comment on posts you can also write recommendations for people and endorse people for skills they can perform. These functions are done against the person's profile rather than appearing on any newsfeed.

· · ·

Instagram

Owned by Facebook (after being purchased by them in 2012), Instagram is a very visual platform. Posts need to be either images or videos and they have attached text which is traditionally filled up with a series of hashtags (there is no requirement to use them, but it's usual to see up to 20 hashtags on a post on Instagram).

Like Twitter you follow someone and they do not need to follow you back. Unlike Twitter it's not clear whether someone is following you back or not, so there's none of the "follow-back" tradition of Twitter. Instagram supports stories like Facebook (in fact they started on Instagram and moved to Facebook) and also live video broadcasts.

Pinterest

Another image-based social media network, Pinterest is a network based on portrait-style image posts. While it seems similar to Instagram the culture on the platform is very different. Most activity is search-based, and hashtags are rarely used. It's much more like a picture version of Google than a normal social network. Clicking on a post will take you to an attached web-site link behind the post, so unlike the other platforms it encourages people to leave the platform. It is also much more likely old posts will be found than on Instagram, where old posts are rarely seen after a few days.

Snapchat

Copied so much by Instagram stories, Snapchat is based on a mix of a story-based temporary 24 hour post format and disappearing messages that you can send on the platform. It's still popular with younger users but has declined in recent years as many people have moved to Instagram.

THE INTERVIEWS

PART I

FINDING A JOB ON SOCIAL MEDIA

INTRODUCTION

In this section I include those parts of the interviews where people talk about the situations where they have managed to receive either a job or clients out of their use of social media.

IT'S INTERESTING that virtually all the people in this section I met via their links to Social Media Examiner's social media content and in person at Social Media Marketing World. The only exception is Deborah Mendes, who I actually met via the original Facebook post, who replied as she saw it shared on Facebook by one of her friends.

1

JEFF SIEH

J eff Sieh is a visual marketing consultant, specialising in Pinterest, Instagram, and video. Jeff is the owner and Creative Director at His Design, Inc. where he has worked to help clients market themselves in the best way possible using a variety of mediums for over 14 years.

He is also "Head Beard" at Manly Pinterest Tips where he is the creator and host of The Manly Pinterest Tip Show.

. . .

WITH TOP TIPS, comedy, storytelling, and just plain fun, Jeff teaches Pinterest techniques like no other. Jeff is also on the Social Team at Social Media Examiner and manages their Pinterest and Instagram as well as appearing in and producing much of their live video content. Visit www.manlypinteresttips.com where Jeff explores visual marketing with character as big as his beard.

JEFF SIEH: What happened is I started my own little show, and I relaunched my show as a podcast called Manly Pinterest Tips, and I was interviewing people. Cynthia Sanchez was big, she had a podcast called Oh So Pinteresting. She was actually working for Social Media Examiner, and I'd had her on my show and all sorts of things, and during this time, I had gone to my first-ever Social Media Marketing World, and I just went to connect with people. I had never been, and I was able to meet people who I had met on all these other social media platforms for the first time in real life, and some of them I had been friends for years.

Jeff Sieh: I went there, and Podcast Movement was doing these one-day events in various cities so the day after Social Media Marketing World, there was Podcast San Diego so I went and stayed on, and went to that, and I met all these other podcasters like Erik Fisher, and some other big ones. And anyway, Erik Fisher and I decided with some other podcasters to form a MasterMind group, so we were in this MasterMind.

Jeff Sieh: Well, I'm doing my show, doing the Manly Pinterest Tips show, and I get a call from Mike Stelzner, and he says, "Hey, I'd like you to be on my podcast." And of course, I wigged out, because I'd been listening to him for a long time, and he was for me the cream of the crop kind of thing to get on. So, went on the show, did okay, I didn't, you know, curse uncontrollably or anything like that. Then I was asked later to be on his Social Media Success Summit and teach. So I did that and then I was offered to speak at Social Media Marketing World.

Jeff Sieh: Around the same time they asked me, because Cynthia was actually transitioning out, to come in and run their Pinterest account. So I had a call with Mike and got that all set up, and then started working for him about the same time as the first Podcast Movement Conference, then I went to speak at Podcast Movement, and then I was asked to speak at Social Media Marketing World, and have been for the last couple of years.

Jeff Sieh: But, getting to run their Pinterest account, eventually I started doing a lot of video with them. I eventually started doing a lot of Instagram, I ran their Instagram account, and then part of the social team, which Erik is the head of and I'm underneath Erik. We work together and we do a lot of live video now, and so a lot of my job now is from Social Media Examiner. I'm still a contractor, I'm not full time, but it's a major client of mine.

Tim Lewis: Yeah, so, if we kind of wind all that back to your initial interview. This really all stems from having Cynthia Sanchez on your podcast. How did you elicit that initial contact with Cynthia Sanchez? Was she somebody you'd heard about on social media? I mean, how did you decide to have her on your show, and how did you approach her to actually get her on your show?

Jeff Sieh: Well, she was really big also on Google+, and she came on the show with the four guys, and then we just kind of developed a relationship. I'd ask her questions. Actually, the first time I went to Social Media Marketing World, we actually did training together, as my company, Manly Pinterest Tips brand, ramped up, and so she was very helpful. But all of that, and then I had contacts with some other people like Peg Fitzpatrick: she was big and helped me out tons connecting with people, like having Guy on my show, Guy Kawasaki, and so all that came from just connecting with people in comments.

Jeff Sieh: They would make a post, I would share it, and I would comment about it, and it was just, it was very organic. One of the mistakes I see a lot of people make is they'll like your stuff, and then a week later they'll go, "Hey, can you share this to all of your followers, and your list?" And that's not the way it happens. It's very organic, it takes a lot of time, and it's just being kind. I mean, it's just being nice.

Jeff Sieh: I mean, Tim, we were connected because you show up almost every time in all the stuff that I'm a part of with Social Media Examiner. I see you in the comments, I see your comments and I laugh at your jokes, most of the time. And there's a relationship that's built over time, but you didn't come on Social Media Examiner or any of my stuff and say, "Oh, that's great, Jeff. Hey, can you be on my podcast?" It didn't happen that way. It took time. It's just like anything else. It's a relationship and a friendship that gets developed and I think that's the only way it can work.

Jeff Sieh: I mean, some of the other gurus teach you how to hit and then do the ask after five times, or whatever. But there's no formula for it, in my opinion. It's all organic and it's just really being kind and being thoughtful on social.

Jeff Sieh: And, you know, when you asked me to come on this, I mean, yeah, no problem. I'd be happy to help, because of that relationship we have developed over time, and conversations we've had, and just being people.

Tim Lewis: Yes, I am looking for patterns in all of this in terms of, I think, it's a mix of intentionality, and, as you say, you have to do it almost organically. And the thing I say to people is that it wouldn't make, for example, any sense for me writing a book about social media if I just went to social media and followed people who were like, musicians or something. You have to be kind of in the areas where the people you are interested in are hanging out.

Tim Lewis: But on the other hand, you're going be connecting with people, and you have to see that there are some people who you will make a connection with. It's like real life. There are some people you're friendly with, and you know, you get on well with those people and it's a good relationship, and there are other people you meet who may be the most wonderfully suitable people for your business, but you just don't connect with them. You just don't have that kind spark of friendship. A lot of the networking guru people are, just like, don't worry that you don't have any connection with this person, really, you don't get on that well. Just thrust your business card into them. And that's where I think they're going wrong.

Tim Lewis: It's like, if you're in the right sort of areas, there will be people that you do connect with, and you do make friends. You have to, as you say, put the time in to actually make friends with people, but it's like, that's where I'm coming from. I think you have to be in the right sort of places, but on the other hand, you shouldn't be just targeting individuals.

Jeff Sieh: It does make sense on some of the numbers. Like Peg Fitzpatrick, she was in my feed because she was providing really good information. The reason she was there and had so many followers was because as she's done that for an extended amount of time, and so it was just natural that I would comment on her posts, because she was putting out good stuff.

Jeff Sieh: But I'm also friends with these artists on Instagram that I met through Google Plus that I still follow to this day, just because their creativity interests me and I support them, and they support me in the best way they can. We talk back and forth and I love it. So it's not just looking at numbers and who can move the needle for you the most. That happens, but find stuff that interests you and that, you know, you can support. It's still fun for me to pop in and find those people on social, and say, "Hey, that is such a cool painting you did. You're so creative," or whatever. And they love that.

Tim Lewis: Also, what I've started to do more recently which is a well-known networking trick, is to introduce people to other people. So, let's say that you have one musician friend who's looking for somebody, and you think they would actually be perfectly suited to connect with this other musician friend who's looking for somebody to do a similar project. It's the same, you never actually do know in the future when you might need a musician friend.

Jeff Sieh: Well, yeah, and it's a funny thing, too. People will come up to you, like, at the conference, and they're like, "Hey, Tim, how you doing? You know, I'm duh-duh-duh." They're just sort of really low key and nice. And then you just happen to go look at 'em, and they're like the number one social media influencer in Australia or something, that you had no idea. That's the kind of stuff that I think is cool, that it doesn't really matter when we get together or why. These numbers are kind of silly, anyway. I mean, some of them, you know.

Jeff Sieh: I would rather be, like you said, introducing people that can help each other out, or provide a service that, hey, I figured out how to do that on video, let me show you how to do that, that kind of stuff.

Jeff Sieh: That's just the way I like to play the networking game.

2

ALISA MEREDITH

A lisa Meredith is the Content Marketing Manager at Tailwind and Founder at alisameredith.com. She enjoys teaching people to use Pinterest (Promoted Pins!) and Instagram ALMOST as much as she enjoys the beach near her home in Wilmington, NC. You can find out more about her at http://www.alisameredith.com

. . .

Tim Lewis: My first category is people who have managed to get a job by making a connection on a social network at their dream company.

Alisa Meredith: So, I'm trying to think of how I first got in touch with Tailwind. I know I was customer before I was anything else, and then actually went to Social Media Marketing World and my friend Vincent Ng brought me to their party. So, I kind of met them in person first, or at least I went to their party, but I don't think I met them.

Alisa Meredith: I'm trying to think how I started talking to them. It's been a lot of years now.

Tim Lewis: How long have Tailwind been going for?

Alisa Meredith: Oh, I should know that. 2012, I think.

Tim Lewis: So, five years old.

Alisa Meredith: Yes.

Tim Lewis: Well, I suppose in some ways, because you were a user of the product, which is a social media product, you found out about the company first on social media. But, I mean, did you ever think that Tailwind would be a great company to work for? Was there a point where you were kind of like, "If they offer me a job I'd take it."? Apart from the obvious you probably need some money, but then the rest of it ...

Alisa Meredith: You know, I haven't really thought about it until this year. I had in the past contacted a couple of people at Tailwind over social media: I had talked to Danny and I had talked to Melissa, and I think I talked to Alex too, because he helped me out with a blog post. I had contacts over social media with them, but I was doing my entrepreneur thing. I was not looking for a job, but I always liked everybody I met at Tailwind, whether it was on social or at Social Media Marketing World. They just seemed like really great people, and I loved the software and I loved the fact that they would never break the rules just to get a new customer, or even a lot of new customers.

Alisa Meredith: So, I felt like it was a trustworthy company that would always take the high road, and I liked that about them. When the opportunity came along, it was just kind of good timing for me, just really thinking about I've been doing this agency thing for a number of years, and so many aspects of it I did not enjoy, that I thought I should look into it.

Tim Lewis: So, was it a case they approached you and said, "We want you to work for us," or was it more you making it known the fact that you maybe wanted to try something different?

Alisa Meredith: Yes. They did not approach me. I'm sure they assumed that I was perfectly content in my own little world. So, when the position became open, I messaged Melissa on Facebook because we knew each other.

Tim Lewis: Yes.

Alisa Meredith: And therefore I would message her on Facebook, ask her a question or something, and I said, "What do you think? You think I should apply?" And she said, "Yeah, go for it. You'd be a great candidate." So, yeah. I applied.

Tim Lewis: From a purely kind of technical point of view then you did apply on social media directly to a person you had met previously.

Alisa Meredith: Oh, yes.

Tim Lewis: Do you think if they'd had no idea who you were and they'd never met you before, that you, even with your outstanding reputation for being the Pinterest advertising expert, that they would have necessarily employed you?

Alisa Meredith: No, no. I don't. But I think that's part of it, right? So, the reputation kind of goes along with it, to be known. I never would have gotten the job if I wasn't known for something, I'm sure of it. But having those connections on social, I felt like we were already kind of friends, especially Melissa.

3

JEN COLE

J en Cole lives in Wichita, Kansas, where she co-owns the social media management firm, DepICT Media.

Jen has a strong passion for writing and building community through storytelling across social media channels for brands and businesses.

. . .

JEN IS ALSO the Community Manager for the San Diego-based company, known as the "authority on social media marketing," Social Media Examiner. You can find out more about her at http://www.depict-media.com

TIM LEWIS: The first category is people who have managed to get a job by making a connection on social media network at their dream company.

Jen Cole: Yeah that's exactly how I got my job. Well, in the long run. It was definitely a journey but yes, I was contacted by Phil Mershon via LinkedIn initially.

Tim Lewis: Presumably he didn't do that sort of cold calling. Was there some sort of relationship between you and Phil that you'd established on LinkedIn before that? Or was it literally a cold calling kind of situation?

Jen Cole: The story's fun because what had happened was I had just accepted a job with RSA Marketing, my first agency job outside my internship. And so I wanted to learn more about social media because I was the only one in the agency who did social media at all. So I signed up for the Social Media Success Summit.

Tim Lewis: Yeah.

Jen Cole: And yeah, I think that was like 2014 probably. I attended the Social Media Success Summit, I got a lot of out the summit, and then shortly after the summit, I got this really interesting LinkedIn message from Phil, that said, "I see that you live in Wichita and you teach Zumba at the same YMCA that my wife goes to." And he goes, "I don't mean this to be creepy but I just wanted to reach out and say hi."

Jen Cole: So that was kind of the beginning of that relationship and we started working on local projects together, like bringing Jeff Sieh to town, bringing Mark Schaefer to town for various speaking events and workshops locally, through a group that is now estab-lished, it was not established back then. Now it is officially estab-lished as Digital Wichita and things happened and I eventually moved on to a bigger agency. But I lost my job with the bigger agency, and then so almost immediately when I lost that job, Phil started offering me positions with Social Media Examiner. But the whole entire relationship started with a LinkedIn message.

Tim Lewis: So it was the fact that you were a Zumba instructor that really got it?

Jen Cole: Yeah, and that's actually the first time I ever started marketing myself on social media, was when I started teaching Zumba. So I was marketing my ability and marketing the events that I would do, marketing my classes so people would come to them, that kind of stuff.

Tim Lewis: So did your LinkedIn profile mention about the Zumba then, yeah?

Jen Cole: Oh yeah it still does, I leave that on there; it's one of the longest jobs I've ever had in my life. Teaching Zumba. I just quit, I did it for five or so years and I just recently let it go.

4

LORI FRIEDRICH

L ori Friedrich is a digital native, despite being from an older generation than normal for people in the digital economy, and enthusiast of all things 'social'. She is passionate about mentoring and coaching, possessing a foundational belief in people. Utilising her 30+ year background in operations management, Lori is a member of the Social Media Examiner event team, leading the content pillar for Social Media Marketing World 2019.

Lori Friedrich: Through a friend, I was able to get an invitation, one of those coveted golden ticket invitations to Google+ when it was still a closed beta program. So, they opened doors on, what was it, June 28th in 2011, and I think I stepped in on July 4th or 5th, something like that. And so, part of the original 500,000 people in there, grew connections organically, and wound up getting connected to someone from the UK who now lived here in the US, and who was putting together a startup, a social startup. And we were talking for a time, while they were trying to get the financing, and I left my job in late 2013, started with them right around Christmas, and was with them until this past spring.

Lori Friedrich: They have changed names now, but it was an absolutely fantastic job because I've been in accounting and operations management for 30 years, and this was an opportunity to come in and run their social media and to be part of the marketing team, something I had a passion for.

Tim Lewis: How much did the company grow while you were there? How much of a dream job actually was it for you joining this startup in a different career area?

Lori Friedrich: We grew from four or five of us past 20. We had people in UK, the US, Ireland, Belgium, all over, and it started to close down obviously, as the money ran out, but the wonderful thing about working there and making the connections I was able to make, and broaden my depth of knowledge while there, allowed me to then, when I left the startup, was to get a job with another social media company.

5

DEBORAH MENDES

D eborah has a business helping companies, consultants and change makers who converse on the topic of The Future of Work get more exposure and reach. She is a turbo connector and uses social media to network and help her grow.

Recently she spotted on Facebook a speaker she knew was speaking at an event. She initiated an enquiry into organising a "visibility hub" at the FreedomXFest Festival in the Pyrenees, where she was able to expand her network with industry leaders in the location independent movement. You can connect with her on LinkedIn.

DEBORAH: I can tell the story of the first time. There were some strange women on Facebook who did live broadcasts. They looked a complete mess. She did it intentionally. Hair was all over the place, and she was called the Get UnStuck Coach, and she lived in this remote part of Canada, I think, but she would continue to do live streams. She had a very infectious laugh, so I liked watching her. She did actually have really good things to say, but her image, you just thought, "Who's this crazy woman?" But that's sort of part of her, and she kind of made it like that intentionally to get people's attention.

Deborah: There was a couple of live streams she did in her dressing gown, but she also had a group which was a community called TeaVolution. It was basically a networking group, and the idea was as if we have a virtual tea with each other, so literally she would just get people in a group by doing these live streams and linking them to another, but I was just very fascinated by how she had made it all work and the networking piece. Then, she submitted, "I'm coming to London," so I just went, "All right, okay. Well, that's interesting."

Deborah: Then it turns out she was having an event on my doorstep; it was just the place I'm always at on the weekends, so that was a kind of, "Oh, right. Well, that's more doable." So, I thought, "Okay, I'm going to go to that event, because it's nearby and that's no effort." Then from there, I met one of the speakers who was then my future sales and business coach for a while. She gave me the idea of my business today, which is getting people in podcasts.

6

CATHERINE CARRIGAN

C atherine Carrigan is a medical intuitive healer, author of eight books and host of the Natural Healing Show for UK Health Radio.

You can find out more about her at
http://catherinecarrigan.com

. . .

CATHERINE: Well, the great thing that happened to me was, as you know, I've published eight books, and I connected with this lovely lady on Twitter and we just became Twitter friends, and I would tweet her, she would tweet me, and she ran the Natural Healing Show on UK Health Radio. So she started interviewing me about my books when they came out. Then recently this year she just got tired of running a radio show and asked me if I would take over it. So to me that's a dream job, if you will. I had my own business for 24 years, I'm an entrepreneur and authorpreneur. But by basically becoming someone's actual friend, then when an opportunity came up to take over this radio show, the Natural Healing Show on UK Health Radio, then I'm the person. So I'm really thrilled about that. So I've done 21 interviews for the show, and it's a great way for me to make new friends in what I do, in natural healing, and also market my business, so it's been a fabulous opportunity and it all came from making friends with somebody on Twitter, of all places.

Tim Lewis: The thing that I'm trying to extract out of all these interviews, when you got this opportunity from the friend on Twitter, was this somebody you connected with on a policy that you were looking to connect with people in your area, or you were looking to connect with particular people in the media in the health and natural healing area? Or was it just a case of it came out of natural conversations that you had on social media?

Catherine: It actually came out of a natural conversation. At the time, if anyone retweeted me or shared my information, I really built my Twitter following on the simple practice of saying "Thank you". I had a programme where if anybody retweeted me, I would write them a personal message just saying, "Thank you for sharing my blog." And I would send them a thank you and a picture of one of my amazing orchids. By doing that I just started making friends. Yara Ghrewati, the original host of the Natural Healing Show, was just somebody that I actually made friends with, and we shared common interests. Then, she has a Facebook group about natural healing, and so she asked me to be a co-administrator of the Facebook group, because I'm interested in that.

Catherine: So first we became friends through Twitter and it just naturally evolved. Then she asked me to co-administrate this Facebook group. Then, again, she was just sort of desperate to find somebody to take over this radio show. She had some personal issues come up and just didn't want to do the work. So she asked me to become the host and take that over for her. I was thrilled. And it all started with a friendship made from Twitter.

Tim Lewis: So you weren't sort of eliciting or trying to say, like, "If you ever feel like not doing the show, then I'll do it." This was something she spontaneously kind of said, "Do you fancy being the new host of the show?"

Catherine: Yeah, it just happened organically, yes.

7

CHRIS STRUB

C hris Strub, CEO of I Am Here, LLC, is a leading voice in the millennial social good space. Chris is the author of '50 States, 100 Days: The Book' about his solo, social media-powered adventure to volunteer with youth-related organisations in all 50 United States in 2015.

Chris has worked with Humana, Big Brothers Big Sisters of America, live-streaming app Live.me, and in 2017, served as a National Red Kettle Ambassador for Salvation Army USA.

. . .

CHRIS'S 'WHY THEN WHAT' online course series, available at www.TeamStrub.com, explains why video should be a critical part of your digital relationship-building approach, and how you can jump-start your video-first networking strategy.

CHRIS STRUB: The last job that I got at Humana was because I made a connection, actually in a Social Media Conference. We talked so much about the social media side of things and following and unfollowing and making connections there, but I actually went to Atlanta, Georgia and met a gentleman named Dan Gingiss in 2014. As we stayed connected through social media, into 2015 and then 2016, eventually that connection turned into a fantastic job for me last year with Humana. I've spoken to Dan, and I feel pretty strongly about this, that it's very difficult these days to get a job if you don't know somebody. Social media gives you a great opportunity to get to know a lot of people, but I think the key that a lot of people miss out on, Tim, is they don't take the time or the effort to develop the relationship to a level where someone would want to offer you a job.

Chris Strub: Social media is not a binary equation. It's not, oh I follow Chris Strub now, and now we're best buds. I value my relationship with Tim a lot more now that we've had a chance to chat, and because he took the time to participate in a project of mine, and so on and so forth, than I do the other 8000 people that I follow on Twitter because again, social media is not a black and white equation. There's a lot more depth and detail and minutiae to these relationships that allow you to get to a point where you can get a job like that.

Tim Lewis: I have got my second part-time job out of social media. I'm gonna be doing some work as a social media examiner. It's just being one of the people who helps with one of their Facebook groups in the European hours. This has come solely out of people that I knew: Jen Cole and she knew Phil Mershon. It's just through these connections that you get. You're right, I think it's changed from the old days where you needed to go down the pub or you needed to basically play golf with the boss or whatever. Now you can get a job somewhere just by the links you have on social media. I think that's something major that's changed.

Chris Strub: I agree 1000%, but I would also add I'm certain that you had quite a few in depth conversations and developed that relationship with Jen and or Phil to get to that point. I think some people reading this or listening to this might think that, oh I'm gonna go follow Jen and that will immediately turn into a job. That's not how it works. You need to take the time, just as with any other friendship in your life or relationship of any kind, to get to know the person, to demonstrate that you care about what they do and who they are and where they live and if they have situations going on with their family or their pets or their significant other. All the answers are there right in front of you.

Chris Strub: When someone is posting an Instagram story or a Snapchat story for the day and they're posting that they're sick or their family member is sick, or they're going to a concert that they've been really interested in for years, these are all critical conversation starters. This is really, as my friend Joe Wilson would say, the artillery that you could use to develop a relationship in a way that will get you to a point where you could get a job. So, social media is not the answer per se, but it's an appropriate start.

Tim Lewis: It's another avenue, I think is the main thing. There have been people I've followed on social media and I've tried to make connections with, and sometimes it's you just don't connect with them. You just don't have that kind of friendship that you build up with other people. So, I don't think I could pick some random person who I want to be friends and just like fawn on their content all the time and guarantee that that would actually give anything, but I think it's a case of just expanding and finding the people that you connect with and going further with that.

Chris Strub: It is, and it's also I've really worked hard over the last three years especially to develop almost a formula to get to know people and to become friends with those people who you want to become friends with. When I met Roberto Blake in Anaheim, we knew each other and he knew me because of the work that I had put in, and vice versa. That he's watched some of my stuff. So while it is relationship based and it's friendship based, there are preferred methods to develop these relationships and if you want to become friends with someone like Joel Comm or Brian Fanzo, it's very doable, but it just requires some effort and some forethought and some empathy. Empathy is the most important thing. Show that you care.

PART II

FINDING ROMANCE ON SOCIAL MEDIA

INTRODUCTION

In this section I include the parts of two interviews where people talk about how they have discovered love via social media. I did have many more interviews arranged with people on this topic but they did not occur due to a variety of reasons. So special thanks to Mark and Julie for offering up their stories.

I met Julie Riley via her connection to Jen Cole and the fact that she often co-hosted Jen's live show with her even before they officially merged their companies to form Depict Media.

I met Mark Orr at the MarketEd.Live conference in Derby last year.

8

MARK ORR

Mark started working with video in the mid 80's and now provides production and editing services for individuals and businesses looking to standout, in the ever growing online world. Mark also teaches you how to make great videos on your phone.

You can find out about Mark at pocketvideoschool.com.

. . .

MARK ORR: I was just sitting one day fed up and just going through some posts on Facebook. I didn't use Facebook a lot, and there was a group of us who had started to connect and meet up face-to-face, as like a mini school reunion, and I hadn't managed to get to the last one, which was December 2010. I couldn't manage to get there for some reason, like I was working or whatever, and there were a few people who'd been and then we were just obviously having dialogue and I just said something, about a few months later, that I needed a holiday 'cause I was working too many hours, and a few people jumped in and said, oh, you should do this, do that, do the other.

Mark Orr: As it happened, I just kind of struck up a conversation with this particular person, and a few things went backwards and forwards. She had come out of a long term relationship, while 18 months prior to that I had been out of a long term relationship for seven years at that point. The conversations just developed on Facebook, and then eventually, speaking by that medium and then dropping phone numbers and speaking to each other over the phone, we could really relate to each other's circumstances because we'd both been in very controlling relationships prior. There was a lot of synergy there about the experiences that we'd had, we both had, grown up kids. And, yeah, just a lot of stuff that resonated with each other, but we had been to school together, you know, we hadn't seen each other for 30 years.

Mark Orr: So, it was interesting to kind of talk about the past and everything and then eventually we decided that we should kind of maybe meet up face-to-face, still no romantic thing at all. It was just a couple of friends who'd been chatting on Facebook, so we did. We arranged to meet at a local garden centre café, and yeah, it was a bit surreal. It was like two friends just chatting, but then we arranged to go for a walk the next day because we were both just a bit fed up of being stuck in the house. Then from that, just from me there seemed to be a bit of a click, and I don't know why. I couldn't put my finger on it.

Mark Orr: And then I text later on that day saying "I felt a little bit differently," which frightened the pants off her, but then she came to see me the next morning on our way to work in a right flap and just asked me what the hell was going on. I said, "Look, this is how I feel, if you don't, that's fine, it's not an issue." But then she thought about it and she thought, well, let's give this a try, so, that was 2011. It was two years later that we decided to actually move in together. So, yes, it was 2013 when we decided to move in together, so my son and I both came over and yes, we're one big family unit now. So, going really well, going strong.

Mark Orr: It's a very different relationship now and I think because of the experiences that we've had. I'm quite open about this now, you've met me in person. I'm a big bloke. I've got a relatively big personality, but I was crushed by this former partner of mine. We were together 16 years, and she basically knocked the life out of me and just made me worthless, or feel worthless, 'cause I couldn't do anything right. Nothing was ever good enough. I had a massive self esteem issue when I came out of that, which was 2004, and it took me a long time to pick myself up. Initially, it was a feeling of euphoria to escape that, but then six months down the line, when I realised that I'd lost contact with all my friends, I didn't really have any family around me, I just had my brother, who I didn't see that often, and I crashed.

Mark Orr: I literally hit rock bottom to the point where I never went anywhere, didn't do anything apart from work. I went to work, but I just had nobody that I could interact with. So, all of those experiences have made us very different people now to what we were. She suffered in a very similar way but not just the mental abuse that I'd suffered but she'd suffered physical abuse. So, we've kind of brought all of this into this new relationship and we've been together, as I say, since 2005, so we're talking six years now, nearly seven, and we've never had an argument all that time. So it's quite strange when you hear people say, oh, no, we never argue, and in the past I would have always cried bullshit. Everybody argues at some point, but we don't, we never do, because we understand each other.

Mark Orr: I think if we'd never had those previous experiences, we would be very different people, 'cause she always says to me, "If we got together 30 years ago, what would it have been like?" And I said, "Probably not what we've got now because we have had all the rest of the shit and the baggage that comes with it."

9

JULIE RILEY

J ulie Riley is the Co-Founder of depICT Media in Wichita, KS and is a Community Manager for Social Media Examiner in San Diego, CA.

She got her start in digital marketing in 2006 promoting an e-commerce program for the company she worked for.

Later she took a job with a local marketing agency where she was able to hone her skills in social media, which allowed her to then leave and form her own agency; which is now depICT Media.

You can find out more about her at http://www.depict-media.com

TIM LEWIS: Please talk about your romantic meetup on MySpace. I suppose you should probably describe how MySpace worked. I've seen it's similar to Facebook. Was there anything specific about MySpace that you liked or disliked?

Julie Riley: It was very similar to Facebook, as far as you had your main page. Some of the things that were nice about it were you could post things, of course, to your page like you would to a wall on Facebook, if I remember right. The note section of Facebook was more of a diary-type section on MySpace. Then the way people would post back to you only showed up on that specific page. There wasn't like a newsfeed with all of the content being thrown onto it. One of the big differences was that if you wanted to see something in particular, you had to go to that person's page.

Julie Riley: I had just moved to Kansas, it was 2006, and I took a job that brought me here. I was living in a duplex next door to a coworker, I was going to work every day. When I'd get off work I was hanging out with coworkers. The only people I was seeing were coworkers, and I was like at some point I have got to meet somebody else outside of this work circle. I worked for Harley-Davidson, I rode a motorcycle, and I was just looking for somebody else who had a motorcycle that knew the roads in the area because, of course, that was before smartphones. I didn't have Google Maps on my phone. If I got lost, I'd better be carrying a pocket map with me to figure out where I'm at. My cell phone, I think, was still a flip phone at the time.

Julie Riley: I went onto MySpace and I started searching for people in the area that had a motorcycle. There was a search feature where you could just look for a male in this age range, in this zip code, and then you could scroll through pictures. Or female, or you could search for people based on certain criteria: age and location.

There were a couple of other criteria, but I don't remember what. As I was scrolling through MySpace, I stumbled across a picture of a guy standing in front of a motorcycle that wasn't a half bad looking guy. But that wasn't my intention. I really was not looking for a guy. Just my odds of finding a guy who rode were a lot higher than finding a girl who rode.

Julie Riley: I looked at his page, and he had a picture of him and his dog, and a picture of him and his son, and said that he was single on his page, because you could have that marked, things like that. I was like, okay. He looked relatively harmless. Of course, this is kind of crazy, but I figured at this point if we met up and he turned out to not be a good guy, I'm on my own bike and I can at least ride away. I'm not in a vehicle with him. I sent him a message and I said hi, this might be kind of crazy, and I promise I'm not some stalker chick. I literally started my message that way. I said I am new to the area, and I saw that you rode a motorcycle and I ride, and I'm really just looking to hang out with somebody who knows the area, and that we can go ride together.

Julie Riley: He sent me a message back and was like, sure, that'd be awesome. Why don't you come to Margarita's tomorrow night? At the time, I didn't know what Margarita's was, because I was literally that new to the area. But Margarita's is a local bar, club. They serve Mexican food, at night they had a band. That particular night I already had plans with a coworker. Imagine that. I was like I can't tomorrow night, I have plans with a coworker. Oh, and in his message when he said why don't you come to Margarita's, we can meet, he said if you see me hugging up on some blonde chick, don't worry, that's Ashley, she's just like my sister. This is our entire meeting. Me saying I'm not a stalker and him saying don't mind the blonde chick. I'm like this is the most bizarre interaction, but I was literally that over my coworkers at that point. I was like I'm going to end up hating my job because I hate my coworkers.

Julie Riley: I said well, I can't. He said, well, there's a ride on Sundays called Cassoday. Cassoday is a town about an hour and half outside of Wichita, and the first Sunday of every month a lot of the bikers in the area would get together, they would all ride to Cassoday; there was a little hole in the wall breakfast place that they would all stop and have breakfast, and then they'd all ride back. It's just something that's been done for years here in the area, and it's always the first Sunday of the month. So I said, okay, sure. He's like, perfect, I'll call you in the morning and I'll figure out where we can meet up. The morning came and the morning went, and there was no phone call. I'm cleaning the house and I'm pacing, and I'm like, at some point, I think it was probably around noon or so, I said this is absolutely ridiculous. I'm 26, there's no reason why I can't call a guy, and why am I sitting here waiting for my phone to ring?

Julie Riley: So I called him. He was still in bed, which is why he never called. Later, after I got to know him, I realised that him saying let's go to Cassoday was like a hilarious joke, because at the time he worked second shift, so he worked from 2:00 p.m. to midnight. He slept in every day, because by the time he got home he'd stay up all night and then sleep most of the day. For him to say he was going to get up in the morning, yeah, that was never going to happen. We ended up saying, okay, let's plan to meet up this afternoon. And he goes, my friend Art is also riding down, because he lived in Derby, I lived in Valley Center, so I lived on the north side of Wichita and he lived on the south side of Wichita in little sub towns outside of the actual city. He said my friend Art lives in Wichita and he's also coming down. Why don't we get the two of you together to ride so he can show you how to get here? I'm like, okay, perfect.

Julie Riley: He gives me Art's number, so I now called, sent a message to Trey and said I'm a random person messaging you. I've now called him randomly, and now I'm calling his friend, Art. The next call is, hi, you don't know me, but Trey gave me your phone number and he said that I should call you because you're headed down to his house and I'm supposed to meet up with you to follow you there. He just laughed and he's like, okay, well do you know where this is? I'm like, nope. I said I know how to get to Alefs Harley-Davidson, and that is it. He's like, oh, perfect. I work across the street from there. Okay, great. So we decided to go meet at Alefs Harley-

Davidson and I followed him down to this place when I thought we were going to Trey's place. Turns out we were not going to his place, we were going to his grandmother's place.

Julie Riley: I walk in the door, before I even meet Trey, I've now met his friend, Art. I walk in, I meet his grandmother, his brother, his brother's girlfriend, a handful of his brother's friends because his brother was in pilot training down in Oklahoma at the time so he was up in town. I meet all of these people, I meet Trey's son. I think he was about eight at the time. I finally meet Trey. So all of that. We went out and it was me, Trey, his friend Art, and then his friend Gary at the time. We all went out riding that afternoon and it was little things. We stopped at Sonic to get a drink in the middle of the day. Trey's like, don't worry, I got it. I'm like, oh, big spender. He bought me a soda. Such a nice guy. Just little funny things. Part of why I moved to Kansas is just to start fresh, and I really, seriously had no intention of dating at that time, getting involved with anybody. I just needed friends.

Julie Riley: We went back to his grandmother's house. They were all barbecuing, had dinner there and decided that everybody was going to go up into town to watch a movie. Anyhow, Trey's son could go to one of them and couldn't go to the other, so his son went with his brother and went and saw the other movie, and then Trey, me, Art and Gary went and saw one movie. What did we see? We went and saw Talladega Nights. After the movie I was going to head home. We were at about the halfway point between his home and my home. He was like, I'm not letting you ride home in the dark by yourself on unknown roads. So he led the way for the most part until we got up into the area where I actually lived, and then I took over. He got there and he was really nice and he said his goodbyes, and said I'll call you in the morning. I was like yeah, sure, I've heard that one. You said that one earlier today.

Julie Riley: The next morning he called and we went and met for breakfast and I don't know, one thing led to another. We ended up seeing more and more of each other over the next couple weeks and it was one of those situations where we really very quickly took the relationship from online to offline, but it was because of online that it even started. Then I remember we were sitting in a bar one evening and the band that was playing was like, if you're single raise your hand. And of course, I'm sitting there in this awkward moment like, well, I'm with somebody but we've never said we're actually together, but I don't think I'm single. And he just looked at me and he goes, you're not single, don't raise your hand. I was like, okay. Well, we got that established. Yeah. He's good about being blunt.

Julie Riley: From there we just regularly started dating and shortly after that, I don't know, probably about a year later moved in, year later we were engaged and got married and had Jett, and it's been really good ever since that. But yeah, it was kind of interesting how, and you know now these people that I met that first day, they're still very, very close. My kid calls Art, Uncle Art. Gary is Uncle Gary. So I got a whole family and friends all at once because I was blunt enough to send one message.

PART III

MAKING IMPORTANT CONNECTIONS

INTRODUCTION

In this section are the interviews where people have talked about where they have received opportunities from social media such as speaking opportunities or finding their ideal VA (virtual assistant).

Again, a large majority of these people I have met via Social Media Examiner's content and in person at Social Media Marketing World, with the exceptions of Denise Cowle, Joanne Sweeney-Burke and Christine Gritmon.

Denise Cowle I met at the Content Marketing Academy Live conference in Edinburgh and I'm not entirely sure where I met Joanne Sweeney, I think it may have been through social connections I had through people in Ireland who knew her. I met her in person for the first time at the Youpreneur conference in London.

Christine Gritmon, even though she was at Social Media Marketing World this year, I didn't actually meet until I was in New York. I'll actually talk about this more in the next section.

10

JOHN KAPOS

J ohn Kapos also known as "Chocolate Johnny" is a third-generation chocolatier and businessman. Hailing from Sydney, he was an early adopter of the online world.

He is constantly keeping up with the latest trends and developments in social media, and knows how to convert that into business success.

During the past four years, he has used social media to take the

"Chocolate Johnny brand" global. His boutique chocolate shop in Sydney is now an international social media dominator.

John is a big fan of live video, which is where the future of social media marketing is predicted to sit. He uses platforms like Periscope, Facebook Live, Instagram Live and Snapchat to build brand awareness while showcasing his delicious products and how they are made.

You can find out about John at http://chocolatejohnny.com/ and his chocolate shop at http://perfectionchocolates.com.au/

TIM LEWIS: How did you get your first speaking gig through social media? Was it a connection you made?

John Kapos: I'd say the first real one where I spoke in front of 400 people, was a guy called Dale Beaumont. He has this really good membership side and he brings in all these people every six months and then he'd talk, tell you about blah, blah, blah. My first speaking gig actually was my own little Instagram conference, one day. 20 people turned up because they didn't have to pay.

John Kapos: I love Instagram as well and I wanted to know who the best Instagrammer was because I wanted to build up my following. I Googled first Instagrammer, anyway, this lady came up constantly on YouTube, her name was Sue B Zimmerman. I just kept on hassling her. If I want something from you, I'm going to nag the shit out of you. You're either going to tell me to go f myself or, "Yeah, come on and talk to me", so I kept on hassling, hassling, hassling. The next thing you know, she's in Australia. I said, "Right, I'm coming to see you".

John Kapos: I messages her and messages, finally she said, "Yeah, you can come and see me, I'm at the Four Seasons Hotel, and I said to her ... I'll bring some chocolate, went in, met her, did a YouTube clip, we did a video, then she said, "Look, would you like to come on CreativeLive? Basically you can do a conference on stage in front of like 20 people, but it's beamed out to thousands, right?

John Kapos: Anyway, she said, "I'm doing an Instagram conference, do you want to come and speak?", so I flew out to San Francisco, I sat in the crowd and one of the sections I got up and spoke. Was that really my first speaking gig? That was in 2014. Yeah, from 8,000 people online, 20 people at the studio.

John Kapos: Then I did SummitLive, so live talking about how to build your brand and business through live video.

Tim Lewis: With those later things like SummitLive, was that a result of that first one you did with Sue B Zimmerman or was that a different connection that kind of got you onto one?

John Kapos: Yeah, it was a different connection, because people watching me on Periscope said, "This guy does it so well", but it's through Sue B Zimmerman I met Kim Garst, I met the Barefoot Entrepreneur, Carrie Wilkerson, who spent $1,000 on chocolates. I met some really amazing people. I met Sunny Lenarduzzi, I got my first podcast interview from CreativeLive with a guy called Tyson Webb, and another guy called Rich Brooks, who was a speaker at Social Media Marketing World.

John Kapos: From there, once you get on one podcast, and everyone hears about you, they go, "Hey, this guy's full of energy, he's nice and he speaks well. Let me get on", and after that, I had more podcasts. Periscope, the Summit Live was because people were watching me. They had their first one in November in 2015. That was their first one, I didn't go, then they asked the crowd, "Who would you like to see as a speaker?" and apparently I got nominated as one of the top three to speak. So that's why they invited me to San Francisco, that was good fun, and then from there I got invited to Social Media Marketing World.

John Kapos: I just came back from New Zealand, my first keynote, so I did two big speeches there. I did San Francisco again. I did something in Spain, so this year's been amazing.

11

JULIA BRAMBLE

W hat does a career developing cutting-edge techniques for forensic science have in common with digital marketing?

Julia Bramble demonstrates that in her work. She converts the best of new technology into simple processes that give results, empowering small businesses to confidently attract clients online.

Julia's approach ('social chemistry') centres on the human behind the digital and forging real connection.

She shares her expertise through training, consultancy and speaking. (She's proud to have presented to audiences as diverse as magicians, local authorities, universities and equine vets as well as those at marketing events including Social Day and Social Media Summit, Dublin.)

Julia is a regular contributor to the acclaimed Social Media Examiner blog.

You can find out about Julia at http://www.bramblebuzz.co.uk (She's also Mum to 6 children and 2 very noisy donkeys!)

JULIA BRAMBLE: Oh, gosh. Where do I start, really? I jump on the #journorequest hashtag: because of that I had a full page in the Observer, featuring myself and my family. I was also featured in the Guardian Small Business feature. They have a Q&A session that's at a specific time. I've done that a couple of times, and that's all been through Twitter.

Julia Bramble: I appeared in an article in the Evening Standard once as a result of an opportunity on Twitter. In that same article was Penny Power, it also featured a quote from her. I was already following her on Facebook, but I used it as an opportunity to ping her and say, "Oh, it's great to see we're in the same article. It would be lovely to have a chat with you sometime."

Julia Bramble: We ended up meeting for a G&T in London, and this was three years ago now, and she told me about the great book Thomas was putting together of social media people, leading social media people, he called it. I never saw that I actually fitted into that bracket. But he was getting together a conference of leading social media people in the UK over a couple of days, so I ended up going along to that.

Julia Bramble: That's where I met people like Timothy Hughes, Gabrielle Laine-Peters and Caleb Storkey, and all sorts of superstars like that, and it was literally from that two days, I think, that I finally got my confidence together around social people, to actually feel that

I could go out there and say to people," Yeah, I'd love to speak at your event, and this, that, and the other."

Julia Bramble: So, I started that summer, and I ended up speaking at Big Social in Manchester, which is where Ian Anderson Gray did his first proper speaking engagement. I'd done a load locally and stuff, and I'd been paid for one before then, but this was actually a social media conference and it was there that I also met Samantha Kelly. Mari Smith was speaking at that one as well, Melonie Dodaro, so it was quite a nice one.

Julia Bramble: But yeah, I met Samantha Kelly and it was because of her that I got to speak, obviously, at the social media summit in Dublin the following year in 2016. And a load of things just kind of flew from there. That's where I met Brian Fanzo for the first time, because he was speaking at that. Steve Dotto spoke at that. Ted Rubin spoke at that.

Julia Bramble: So, all of a sudden, new worlds completely opened up, and that's led to all sorts of opportunities. That was all from replying to things on Twitter and just talking to journos on Twitter and just looking for opportunities on Twitter. That all sprung from there. And basically that two days, with Penny and Thomas Power, spring boarded everything else. Which is why I'm really happy to support Penny now in her crowdfunding for her business adventure, because she's helped me so much. And they didn't realise it at the time. Of course, they didn't, because they're really humble people, but yes, it was amazing.

Tim Lewis: So, if we wind back, you mentioned #journorequest, which I know is basically a hashtag that journalists use mainly on Twitter, I guess, I don't think they use it anywhere else, but put in requests, I'm looking for somebody to do something. When did you first become aware of the #journorequest hashtag, and were you systematically looking at every day, or every couple of hours, or something? When did you first think, "Oh, maybe I should look at this"?

Julia Bramble: I think I heard about it quite early on, actually. I've been doing this since like 2010, and it's definitely been around since 2011 ish, because I know that it was pointed out to me.

Julia Bramble: But I was probably systematically doing it for about a year. No, maybe six months, before I got that opportunity. But that opportunity for that particular article, I think actually came from me chatting with somebody who turned out to be a PR person, and also the opportunity for me, which was nice.

Julia Bramble: But I've lots of other things that have sprung out of the #journorequest. I actually got paid to write about 300 words for Bella Magazine, I think. I got paid for that. It was nice. I was featured in House Beautiful, which is crazy, isn't it? And I had another little piece in the Guardian, all about how to jump onto trending topics and make the most of them, and that just started off a broad conversation about business books you should read and things like that. So, yeah, just loads of stuff has come out of that. So, that's a really big one for people.

12

CHRISTINE GRITMON

C hristine Gritmon helps the busy owners of small, local businesses be less intimidated by social media. Her previous experiences includes marketing work for big-brand beauty, local journalism & newsroom engagement work, and creating funny Photoshops for a comedy website (yes, really). She lives with her husband and two small children in Nyack, NY. You can find out about Christine at http://www.gritmon.com/

. . .

CHRISTINE: So first of all, when I first started my company, which was in 2016 when I first quit my job and started Christine Gritmon Inc., Inbound was the first conference I knew about, and the first conference I attended. I actually had a terrible time at the first one for various reasons unrelated to the conference itself and I knew that they were unrelated to the conference itself, and I knew that the conference itself was still great. I learned a lot of great things even though I was on the most basic ticket to keynotes. So, I did return the following year.

Christine: But even still I remember at the 2016 conference I said, "I'm going to speak at the 2019 conference." I just kind of had that as a goal, and I didn't even know what I would speak about 'cause I was new. I said, "But you know, I want to." I knew I wouldn't be on the keynote stage, for the breakout sessions. And I didn't get to attend with the breakout sessions, since I was on the basic ticket. But anyway, I'm usually a very strong networker. I didn't even really chat with anyone at that conference. I was just ... it was just kind of a weird time.

Christine: So then, 2017 I had a much better time at the conference. But more importantly, I learned something shortly before going to it that I didn't have a chance to put into action yet for 2017. But I have already for 2018 and it's doing wonders: someone who I met at Social Media Marketing World 2017, which is now a much bigger conference in my world, Brian Fanzo, appeared on my Facebook show. He talked about how to really get the most out of conferences and appearances. And one of the really big things that stuck with me was pre-networking. I had always done a bit of pre-networking shortly before the conference, and during the conference, and seeing who was using the conference hashtag on Twitter. I mean, that's kind of the only place I really did it.

Christine: But I started doing that with InBound for this year. First of all, I've already been connecting with people using the hashtag. But second of all, while I was at Social Media Marketing World this year, I connected with a lot of people. I connected with a ton of people at that conference. One of the people I connected with, Holly Chessman, she is from Boston. I said, "Oh, do you go to InBound?" She said, "I go to InBound ever year. I'm applying to speak this year." I said, "Oh, I didn't see the call for speakers. How do you apply to speak?" And she said, "Oh, I'll forward you the email." She sent along the email, and I applied. I submitted two submissions, two different topics, and one of them got picked. I will be speaking about how to use video on social media, at different points of the sales funnel.

Christine: But, I'm crazy excited. It's the first time I'll be attending not on the super basic, "you only get into the Keynotes" ticket. And most importantly, and in addition to the fact that I'm excited that I'll be speaking, I have connected in advance with several people who will be there. This is the first time I'm going to walk into that conference and have people I'm looking forward to meeting up with which is very exciting. And which is only going to grow because now the conference is in September so July is really when I'm going to hit that hard and really try to pre-network and connect with people not only on Twitter but also people who have been talking on the events and the page and on Facebook, Instagram and LinkedIn.

Christine: Another really big thing I'm going to be doing now is I'm going out to Inbound and we don't get paid to speak. We get access to a nice fat discount at a fabulous hotel but we don't get paid to speak. So I'm going to pay my way there via putting together some paid speaking opportunities hopefully locally. It would have been right before the conference but that's Labour Day so it'll be right after the conference. I know a lot of people in the Boston area including the aforementioned Holly who I know from Social Media Marketing World who will be at Inbound. So we're hopefully going to put together some sort of workshop or something in the Boston area while I'm out there anyway.

Christine: And I have another friend who I met on social media. This guy, totally different connection, I met through my college alumni network. There's a guy on Twitter who likes connecting with other alumni of our college. This guy Clay, he connects with lots of

Vassar alumni. He connected with me and he connected with this guy Bruce. And Bruce also works in the social media space and lives in Boston. So Bruce and I are going to try to put something together as well.

Tim Lewis: One thing I would ask and I've asked other people but I suspect you'll have a better idea than a lot of people. You say about pre-networking at conferences. You're ideally doing that via social media. What would you say your methodology is in terms of how you do that?

Christine: There's a couple things I do. One of them is very simple. I literally go on Twitter and type in the hashtag of the conference. So right now I've gone and typed in #inbound18 and anyone who is using it in the proper way like saying, "I'm excited to go, I'm excited to speak, etc." - I'm adding them to a list and when I feel like specifically engaging them on a topic I can go look at that list. I'm bad at that part.

Christine: But the fact is, people see I've added them to a list. A lot of times if the post is really about the conference I will comment and say, "Yes, I'm so excited to see you there." One person who's actually presenting on a similar topic I commented said, "oh, well awesome. I'll be presenting on a similar topic." And told them what I'd be doing and then some other people commented on that and said, "oh, I want to check that out." I said, "oh, please do." And so I've connected with those people. So Twitter's really, really a great place to start that in that regard.

Christine: Another thing that's really a basic thing to do ... Inbound has over 250 breakout sessions, so I don't quite do this with Inbound. But with Social Media Marketing World I often do this. I'll look at the list of speakers and I will follow them on Twitter and if they have a Facebook professional page I'll like it. I don't friend them unless I know them, generally. Though they sometimes friend me and I say fine. I'll often add them on LinkedIn and I'll send a message and I'll say, "Hey, I saw you are speaking at this conference. I'm attending, looking forward to hearing you speak."

Christine: People have different feelings on LinkedIn. Some people will say, "Okay, great. That person I should network with." And they'll add me and that's great. Some people like Mike Stelzner from Social Media Examiner, for example, he will not add you on LinkedIn if he doesn't feel like he knows you. He has met me numerous times but I haven't stuck in his head yet so he is not on that app with me. And that's fine too. I don't take it personally if people don't add this person they don't know. But that's what I do. I just reach out. I make these contacts. I get in touch and hopefully a lot of times they are sufficiently intrigued to also become aware of what I'm doing and sometimes they're not and that's fine. Because it's really about me being open towards them. They are the identified kind of leaders which is why they are on the speaker list and whatnot.

Christine: I also have my fellow attendees of conferences ... the conversations happening by using a hashtag. Because I remember before Social Media Marketing World '18, when I did that search of the conference hashtag, if it was talking about the conference, I found Chris Strub who was a fantastic find. He's very much a community builder and connector, so he was having a conversation and Zala was on it and Ai was on it and now I talk to them all the time. So I found people via a conversation that he was hosting and now I know these people in real life. Now I'm doing work with these people. I'm appearing on their work, they're appearing in mine. It's really lovely and we're also we're crazy excited to actually get to meet each other at the conference. It's nice to walk into the conference and be like, "Oh, I've had conversations with this person, and I know that they're good to know."

Christine: But then also we were super excited to meet up next year. Ai is a good example. Ai Addyson-Zhang, I met her through that conversation or possibly not even that conversation. Possibly I think she was just a hashtag search as well. I searched the conference hashtag and I found her. She's fantastic. We became good Twitter friends before Social Media Marketing World when we met at the happy hour the night before. We were very excited to meet each other and we stayed in touch throughout. And I wound up connecting her to a mentor of mine, Sree Sreenivasan. He's not part of the Social Media Marketing World crowd but he is a big deal on social media especially in the areas of education, journalism, and culture. And Ai works in the education space with social media. So that was a good connection.

Christine: And now they have done things together. Ai came out last month to Sree's big event for the year which is Social Media Weekend in New York City. She was a speaker. And she co-presented with one of Sree's main collaborators: it was fantastic that she made these connections and now she's doing other stuff with Sree and I'm really, really excited that my simple act of just searching a hashtag for a conference has led me to helping some really great people connect. Because often-times I know people who don't know each other but they really should. So it's really satisfying to see those connections get made and to be part of it.

Tim Lewis: So I suppose for the reader you have got this huge number of people on the hashtag you were tweeting. Do you make the decision as to who to spend the time on, who to develop the relationship with as opposed to somebody not to develop that relationship with. So what kind of identifiers do you use to work out who, not so much as to who's important, but rather who you want to focus your attention on?

Christine: I'm changing my stance on this, changing my approach to this. Earlier on, when I didn't really know a whole lot and I wasn't really solid on who I was in this space, not that I am now, but when I was new I kind of chased the shiny things. I said, "Okay, so this person's name comes up a lot. They seem like a good person to be in with." And that especially changed with my experience this past year at Social Media Marketing World because a lot of the people who I wound up really making valuable connections with weren't the speakers, they were the volunteers.

Christine: I didn't realise that volunteering at the conference was actually such an honour and that a lot of these people, it's not just the college kid giving free high fives, there's also people who are really, really advanced social media marketing professionals who are also helping you get from place to place and volunteering at this thing.

And those turned out to be a lot of the best people to get to know because the mere fact that they were cool with doing that said something about them as people and what it says is that they're more interested in being a part of something than they are in being center-stage. And a lot of them are perfectly capable of taking center-stage and they do in their professional lives.

Christine: But when it came down to it, they were excited to contribute to this community. And those are the people I want to hang with. Even some of the bright shiny speakers like Andrew and Pete, they've been speakers two years in a row and they are so about chatting people up and giving back and they remember who you are. And you register on their radar even if you are not in a spotlight. Those are the people I really, really like.

Christine: Brian Fanzo's got a bit of that going on. I'm about to see him. Julie and Jen are amazing because they are behind the scenes for the Social Media Marketing World stuff. They're at their laptops. But they are a big deal. And the fact that they are just so approachable and cool and fun and they're people who don't care that you don't have a million followers and still find you worthy of conversation. Those are the good people. So I'm really shifting my focus and looking less at whose name appears a lot of places and more at who's engaging in conversations with the people who I know are givers.

Tim Lewis: Now I think that's very similar to how I would treat it.

Christine: They care more about the nice kids than the cool kids.

Tim Lewis: I'm not saying that anybody else is horrible or sacrifices kittens or whatever. But it's a case of, with networking and social media networking especially, it's basically who gels with you personally that matters. It's like with people trying to get a job at another company. I've talked to a few people who've got jobs from social media. You can't say, "Oh, I want to talk to this particular person who's the CEO of Google," or whatever. But you can say, "I'm interested in people in that kind of job."

Tim Lewis: You can't say for a specific individual that you want to make a connection with them because that's very hard. Because you just don't know if you're going to gel with a person. The chances are you're going to be able to gel with somebody around that level. But you can't say a specific, "Oh, I want to be friends with Chris Strub." or "I want to be friends with Brian Fanzo," or whatever. You have to say, "This is the kind of person I'm looking for." And then you need to be aware of that. And those are who you are looking for connection-wise.

Christine: Also, the fact that it's the ability for these connections to enrich your life. You can look at it in different ways. There's people who I really follow and I look at all the work they do and I want to connect to. I'm not going to name names. But there's someone in particular I can think of where I was like, "I kind of want to do what that person is doing. And I'd like to get into that space. And that person has courses," and all these things. And I was thinking, "Oh, I got to get to know that person." But, that person has a lot of boundaries in place. And it doesn't make them a bad person but the fact is they have boundaries in place and they're not really interested in getting to know everybody. They want to do their thing and the people who are in their circle are in their circle. And it's not an exclusivity thing. It's a matter of just managing their own energy. Because if they decided to become best friends with everyone who admired them, that's exhausting.

Christine: So they have just drawn those barriers in their own lives. And I realise it's not a bad thing. That's perfectly valid. But at the same time, I need to not go into environments saying, "Well, I don't care. It's my goal to get in with that person." What does it get me? It gets me a fancy friend and maybe it gets me ideally some mentorship but that's not what they're interested in so probably not. What do I want out of a relationship? And I also have limited emotional bandwidth. So I want the people who are going to energise me.

Christine: A good example of this is where I was thinking about going into this Road To Social event where I'm going to be with a dozen other social media people. Some of whom I know already. Some of whom I don't. I thought, "What am I most excited about?" And I realised, I'm most excited about hanging out with Jen Cole,

Julie Riley, and Chris Strub. Because they're people where, if I decided tomorrow this whole being a social media strategist thing is just not working out, I'm going to give it all up, I'm going to go get a day job somewhere I'd stay in touch with those three. I would want to still hang with them and I have their numbers in my phone now, those are the people I'm keeping, not just because of our shared profession. That's how I met them but I want to keep them regardless.

Christine: I'm just shifting focus to that because I'm realising there's a lot of people who can help me professionally. But I'm kind of gravitating now more to people I want to hang with. That's harder to find and it's a more specific thing. And you can't really over plan that because you don't know who you're going to gel with. The fact that they do something similar to what you do doesn't necessarily mean that they are an asset to you.

Tim Lewis: So, is there anything else that you want to add in terms of how to do live tweeting at a conference for example? That certainly is something I'm quite interested in.

Christine: The first time I realised how much visibility and how much value it could give you to be one of the top users of a conference hashtag, was at a much smaller event. It was at Social Media Day Mahwah in northern New Jersey. It was a suburban thing. The following year it actually became one of my first presentations which was cool. But the first year I went I just started live tweeting peoples's sessions that I attended. I had been a journalist previously and I had learned about live-tweeting events with journalism. So I went to this event and I sat through peoples's great sessions at Social Media Day Mahwah. And I tweeted the heck out of them. I tweeted out selfies with people and all these things using the conference hashtag. They had big screens at the conference that were tracking the hashtag and showing tweets of people using the hashtag. A lot of conferences do that now. Inbound does it too.

Christine: And I found myself getting a bit competitive. I love the fact that I was always on there. In fact, I took a picture at one point of a screen that was all me which isn't ideal. But it was kind of cool. I walked in not really knowing people and people not knowing me and by the end everyone wanted to know who I was because they were following my tweets.

Christine: And that was the first time I experienced that. The first time I experienced, "Wow, I can become known simply by sharing the insights I'm getting from others." I'm still in touch with and have worked with people who I met at that conference. My business coach is someone who I met at that conference. I didn't wind up working with her until a year and a half later but it was very cute. The following year I wrote to them at some point. I said, "So, how do people submit and apply to speak at this year's conference?" And they said, "Oh we definitely want you." I was like, "You know who I am?" They said, "Of course, you made a big impression last year." Sure enough, even though I was a speaker at the following year's one, I was also the top tweeter. I won a prize.

Christine: There are some other people I've put together with speaking opportunities and podcasting opportunities and things of that nature, who I met at that very first event which I walked into as a totally unknown entity. Just connecting on social media, sharing what I was learning, people got that impression of me. First of all, she is someone who is at a place where she's learning all these insights, so she's developing her skills. And second of all, she's someone who wants to share it. And that's something I always want to be known as. I always want everyone to win. I don't want to hoard my knowledge. And I realise that there's a lot of benefit that can come from things of that nature. So I do that at every conference now. I'm very competitive about being on the leaderboard. I'll be at a conference with five thousand people and if I'm not in the top ten people using the hashtag, I fire it up. I do some additional thumb exercises and do a few shots of espresso and get my head in the game and get back up there.

Tim Lewis: I so want to do this: there's a few people in the UK I know who are totally competitive with the live tweeting thing. I so want to arrange a conference and invite you and them just to have a competition as to who can be the top tweeter.

Christine: That is how I met Holly. Holly who I'm now going to be hanging out with in Boston and putting a workshop together with when I go out for Inbound. I met her because she was the top tweeter and we were competing and I made sure to find her. I sought her out and I said, "We need to get a selfie of us together and tweet it out to show." She beat the crap out of me. She did much better than I did. She earned that. And similarly, at Inbound the previous year, I'm surprised I didn't see Holly on that tweet list because she was also a big tweeter at Inbound. But I met someone who I wound up having as my guest on my Facebook Live Show a few weeks later. I'd be the top tweeter of that conference, because clearly they're of my ilk.

Tim Lewis: Okay, so this is something I do a fair amount. I'm really not at your level of live tweeting at conferences and I certainly didn't do it this year at Social Media Marketing World. But what would you say to people who were like, "Well, I'm struggling to write notes of the conference that I'm looking at. I'm looking at trying to understand what the conference person is talking about. How do I get time to tweet: what sort of things should people concentrate on when they're doing live tweeting?" What are your tips for live tweeting at conferences?

Christine: Get the essence and if you don't get the exact wording, literally nobody, not even the presenter, will care. As long as you properly get the essence of what they're saying. If you cut out an "and" or "the" nobody will care as long as the value of what's being put out there is being appropriately conveyed. I've actually had speakers write to me after their talks and say, "You captured what I said better than I said it. God bless you. This is of tremendous value to me." Then I got on their radar which was nice. If you focus too much on the exact word, three more wonderful gems of knowledge are going to fly right over your head while you're fiddling with your keyboard. So just get it out quick.

Christine: Another thing I always, always do, this is a big tip is on the notes on my phone, the little Notes app, I make sure to preload it with the Twitter handles of the speakers and the conference hashtag. So then when it's time for the session I just copy that bit and I just paste it at the end of each tweet. It saves me seconds but boy do they add up. So that's a huge tip. Make sure that you have loaded up on your copy paste the speaker's handle and the conference hashtag.

Christine: Another thing is I just discovered a few conferences ago that I've apparently learned how to type double thumbed. So one thumb handles one end of the keyboard, the other handles the other. And it's much like when I learned how to properly type on a keyboard, in about fourth grade. I had been typing all along and I was really fast at finding the keys with my fingers. But once I learned where things were to a different level and got that rhythm, I'm a speed typer now. It's ridiculous. So that has also really helped.

13

DENISE COWLE

D enise is a copy-editor and proofreader based in Glasgow. She specialises in non-fiction, particularly education and business, and edits for a variety of global publishers, companies and organisations.

She is an Advanced Professional Member of the Society for Editors and Proofreaders, and in September 2017 she was elected to its council as Marketing and PR Director. You can find out about Denise at http://www.denisecowleeditorial.com/

. . .

Denise Cowle: The opportunity that I thought of was the one which was meeting Chris Marr through Periscope and getting to know him just a little bit and some other marketing people, and he ran a competition to win a ticket to the CMA conference in September 2015, and I won that.

Denise Cowle: So I won the ticket to the conference, which also included a workshop the day before with Marcus Sheridan, who I'd never heard of, and I didn't know what content marketing was and I just, to be honest, felt a bit of a fraud winning the ticket because I thought, "I don't see how this can possibly be really relevant to me because I'm an editor and what has content marketing got to do with me?" But I thought, open to new ideas, I'll go along, I might get a client or two, you never know, and that has completely changed my business in the last two years. There's no question about it. It's just changed absolutely everything which is quite scary when you think about it.

Tim Lewis: What was the take away you had from that first CMA event? Did you start a blog or something along those lines?

Denise Cowle: I did. I went away and I blogged because the workshop that Marcus did was an introduction to content marketing. Now, up until then, as a freelance editor and proofreader, when I look back on it, it was very much a gig approach that I had to my business, just about taking work of all kinds and just going from one gig to the next almost, and hoping that you were going to have enough work and not thinking, well definitely not thinking, of it as being a business owner.

Denise Cowle: So I didn't really know if marketing, and this is laughable now Tim, it really is, I didn't really know if marketing would be relevant to me. Just, "Do I really need to do this?" and spending that day, I think it was a half day or we started late morning with Marcus's workshop, it was like the scales falling from my eyes.

Denise Cowle: Because when he was talking about content marketing and pricing and things like that, and he was saying, "Well, I know what you're going to say. You're going to say that, oh this is very interesting, but it doesn't apply to my business because what I do is different and we are special." And he basically just blew all that out of the water and said "You have clients out there that need information. Why wouldn't you give it to them? And this is how you do it." It was such an eye opener. It was incredible.

Denise Cowle: Then the next day we had speakers, Stefan Thomas came, and Gavin Oates and a few other different people and I just thought "Shit, I really should be doing this. This is absolutely crazy." So I did go and start a blog. It was a bit of a false start because I hadn't thought enough about who I was blogging for but I started : I only did a few, maybe about half a dozen, with much more of a physiotherapist approach.

Denise Cowle: So things like health at work, sitting and standing and stretching at your desk, all that sort of thing. But then I completely rethought that and thought "No, this is not talking to my clients." So that really got me into thinking about blogging and doing that and then attending, staying still on the periphery of the CMA really. I wasn't a member at that point, but I was using their free content and I was in touch with them, and I went to the conference in 2016 and I joined the community after that.

Denise Cowle: It's just been completely different for me, running my business. See now I say running my business rather than working as a freelancer.

Tim Lewis: Yes.

Denise Cowle: It's two different mindsets so it has completely shifted my mindset.

Tim Lewis: And how did you end up watching that Periscope broadcast in the first place. What attracted you to Chris Marr?

Denise Cowle: Well, it's a weird thing because, as you probably gathered, I am not an early adopter. I'm not in there with these things. And I had a look back to see, and Periscope, I think, launched in about March of 2015. I think I went on to it first around about June of 2015, and I honestly can't remember what brought it on to my radar, but I was obviously curious enough to go and have a look. And then, just by chance, somebody was broadcasting from Loch

Lomond, which is obviously just up the road, and I've clicked on to her Periscope, and it was a woman called Liz Melville. She's a social media marketer, she's based up Loch Lomond way. She does a lot of Facebook stuff actually.

Denise Cowle: I just started following her just to see what she was doing round about Scotland, but of course she was being followed by other marketers, and through her I met Chloe Forbes-Kindlen, and Chloe said, "You should follow Chris Marr". And it was her that put me on to him. She was a social media marketer as well. She's been to a couple of CMA events, although she wasn't there this year.

Denise Cowle: It was her that said, "Follow Chris". I didn't really know why, but then I did start following him. He was quite compelling on Periscope, and so I started following him on Twitter as well, and various other channels, and in Blab. And I was just inter-ested in what he was saying and how he was talking. It was all just so new to me, it was like a whole door opening up to a different world really, this whole marketing malarkey that I'd never really thought of at all.

Denise Cowle: It's astonishing when I think back. I don't know how I thought I was going to get work. But do you know, Tim, so many editors and proofreaders still work on that gig basis and they really don't think about how to get clients and how to market them-selves strategically and properly. But I think it's changing. Louise Harnby, who you know, Louise and John Esperian did a content marketing session at our conference this year. It's interesting just to see how many people are becoming more visible online, on the back of that, definitely. People starting to think about saying things publicly and putting their opinion out there and doing a blog and upgrading their websites and stuff. It's good.

14

IAN ANDERSON GRAY

I an Anderson Gray is the founder of the Confident Live Marketing Academy and Seriously Social. He's an international speaker, trainer, teacher, web developer and consultant. He helps business owners level up their impact and authority by confidently using live video. Ian is co-founder of Select Performers – a family run web agency. As well as being a geek, husband, and dad to two kids, Ian is also a professional singer and lives near Manchester in the UK. You can find out about Ian at http://iag.me/

· · ·

IAN: Yeah, it's kind of weird the way this started, but I was, particularly three or four years ago, really active on Twitter. Not so much now, but at the time I was. I made a lot of connections internationally, but also in my own city of Manchester and there is this company called Pro-Manchester, which was putting on all these events to do with social media and marketing and helping businesses. I got noticed as somebody who seemed like I knew what I was talking about when it came to social media and they brought me in to speak at local events in Manchester. Following on from that, they then were wanting to put on a big social media event too, which was kind of billed as the UK equivalent of Social Media Marketing World, and it was called The Big Social Media Conference. They asked me to speak at that.

Ian: That kick started everything really for my speaking career because at that event, where they invited some big names from the US such as Mari Smith and from Canada, Melonie Dodaro. That's how I also met Julia Bramble for the first time.

Ian: Yeah, that was my first kind of big speaking engagement. It all came about through actions on Twitter. So that was a massive thing.

Ian: I have to say that I had probably been on Twitter for about six or seven years prior to that, let's see, at least. And these relationships could be building over a number of months and years. It wasn't like an overnight change, but certainly that was my experience.

Tim Lewis: Was it somebody who you'd built a relationship with on Twitter who invited you? Did they actually invite you on Twitter or was it an email sent referring to the fact that they knew you on Twitter or all the rest of it?

Ian: Yes, that's a really good question, particularly with Twitter. Twitter is a very fast moving social network and it's also one where it's usually a good conversation starter, so that's where the connections start. So, I made some connections with these people, with the guys of Pro-Manchester, through Twitter. Actually, the main guy, I didn't really have a proper conversation with him. He was, I kind of found this out later, he was almost like, not stalking me, but he was consuming my content, but not really interacting with me, which was interesting. I think we tend to talk a lot about these two-way relationships, but quite often you just being active on Twitter, you can be noticed. They're almost like lurking in the background. If that makes sense.

Ian: So, yes. In answer to your question, actually being asked to speak didn't happen on Twitter, but the conversation and the relationship started on Twitter and then they moved on to traditional things like email and conversations and actually meeting in person.

15

SHELLEY RÖSTLUND

S helley Röstlund is a digital consultant with a specialism in the use of social media within the web, marketing and communications space. She runs a digital agency in Northampton (UK), providing consultancy and management solutions for SMEs (Small and Medium Enterprises). You can find out about Shelley at http://www.mysocialintelligence.com/

. . .

TIM LEWIS: So the next category is any great opportunity that people have got via a connection they developed on social media, and I think this is where your VA (Virtual Assistant) falls into.

Shelley: I think so, yes. I mean, because she also does a lot in the social media space in terms of a VA, she showed me quite early on what she was able to do for other clients. But then I was doing franchise consulting, then I shifted into digital, which is what we'd been doing now for seven years. But what was really useful with that relationship is we met on Twitter, then you have your Skype conversations as well, and you just take it off social media, but you do continue it a little bit.

Shelley: She quite early on helped me understand how to actually outsource a certain amount of the administration behind social media. And actually helped me in the early days really on my product development.

Tim Lewis: So when you met on Twitter, were you looking for a VA, or was she just somebody you were talking to on there? Did you tweet something and she responded? Was she looking for somebody to work for, or was it just a case of you had started a conversation, and then it's like, "Well, what do you do?", and it went on from there? How did it work?

Shelley: Yes I think it was just organic. I think again like I say, it was 2009, so there was a lot less noise, it was a lot easier to find humans. I think that what's nice about the way Kirsty tweets and still does today, is that she's very personable within her content. And actually her content's quite useful. I think because she's a bit of a traveller at heart, so she spends a lot of time taking short breaks around Australia. She's based in Melbourne. So I think that kind of appealed to my adventure spirit as well. It was like oh great, and then you have something to talk about as well. I think it's finding those commonalities.

Shelley: Then I did get a bit more interested in it. Because I was learning more about the space of actually being able to outsource and have remote workers, that kind of spurred me into, "Let's have a

Skype, let's have a chat, tell me what it is that you do." Because I kind of got to know her a little bit through Twitter, and then we took it off Twitter to get to know each other better. So I think it was more about her, the way she tweeted, just always quite personable, her name is there. So it's not a brand, it's Kirsty, so you get to relate to that person a lot quicker.

Tim Lewis: As well as having all the anecdotes and stories in the book, I am trying to get to how these kind of relationships start. I mean, the central theme as far as I can tell is that most people weren't looking for anything in particular. They were just looking to make connections and make friends with people. And then these things came as a result of things beyond that.

Shelley: Yes, I think depending on when you started, if we're only talking about Twitter, I think depending on when you actually started with a particular platform, it's what the environment was like a little bit at the time as well. Whereas now if you met someone on Twitter, it probably had to be a little bit more strategic perhaps, or someone might have referred the person.

Shelley: Do you know what I mean? So I think that was a little bit as well, because I could see a lot of people talking about her as well, going, "Oh, you know, Kirsty you're my angel, you're my this and that." I thought oh, she must be good. And actually, she gets about 70% of her business through Twitter referrals. So she's very good at keeping that organic kind of conversation going anyway. She's been in business now for 12 years, so it helps the longevity of your business as well.

Tim Lewis: Have you ever systematically looked for a connection to do a particular activity on social media? I mean, say if you were looking for an email specialist or something. Have you ever been in the situation where you thought, "Oh, I'll try and use social media to find somebody like this?"

Shelley: Well, the only way I would use social media in that respect is because we've done quite a bit of streamlining and systemizing in our business in the last 18 months, and also product diversification. Which means that I have to go and find the kind of partners that I want to deal with. But I don't outwardly shout out, going, "Hey, hey, look! Who does email, email, email?"

Shelley: I try not to do that, because what I value more is actually let's say does Tim know someone, because for me in my head, because in the industry that he's in, when Tim uses an email guy, that email guy will be particularly good because they will have to have done these particular things. So I prefer to either go into a niche social media group, like a Facebook group. I don't use LinkedIn. I only Facebook for groups. And I will ask for that, and then have a bit more of a conversation, and then I will go and find that person and try and connect with them or ask for an introduction.

Shelley: So again, I still want to qualify people because there's loads of people that, as you know, in my industry, digital, who are perceived an expert or a guru, or something like that. But for me, the proof is in the eating of the pudding, not the making of it.

Shelley: So while some people might know certain things, because our approach is quite holistic. We work in an ecosystem, I like to know that whoever I'm trying to reach out to can tick a few more boxes where they understand the ecosystem, and they're not just, "Oh, this is what email was like 15 years ago, and this is the only way we do it," and it's the same for SEO, the same for a website. It's the same for all of them. So I think when I'm trying to go out to find those people, I will try and seek you out and potentially I'll go, "Oh, who does Ian Anderson Gray know or who does so-and-so know." But actually then qualify them even more. So I'd probably go niche within social media.

Tim Lewis: Yes. Well, I actually think if you approach five or six people and said, "Who is the best person you think for this activity?", and they just all say the same person that's the person you go for?

Shelley: I mean, when there's communication, okay maybe that's someone to talk to, but I'm also a bit wary of in the digital age that we're in, the first name that comes to mind for many people is because they happened to be the smartypants that was a speaker at six events. But the best person's not necessarily the speaker that is speaking at six events. So while I enjoy going to events, and the hard work it takes to become a speaker and all those things, I don't necessarily qualify their expertise on whether they got to be on a stage or not.

JOANNE SWEENEY

J oanne Sweeney is the founder of the Digital Training Institute and Public Sector Marketing Pros. She's a skilled digital marketing consultant and trainer. Her clients include the largest political grouping in the world and Google.

Joanne is a published author and is currently writing her second digital marketing book. She also hosts a weekly podcast called JSB Talks Digital.

Her writing has been published on Social Media Examiner and Joanne has spoken on stages in the US, mainland Europe, the UK and Ireland.

JOANNE: Oh, yeah. So this is my favourite story when I'm talking to people who are not convinced about Twitter. I was writing my book two years ago and, obviously, I was looking at who were the influential leaders in law enforcement and social media and there is a dedicated hashtag for that. It's #LESM, law enforcement social media, and very quickly it became clear to me that Lauri Stevens was actually the influencer in this space and there weren't a whole pile of other influencers.

Joanne: So, obviously, I was following her, and I remember the Sunday night in the winter when we were watching a show after the 9:00 news at prime time I got a ping on my phone and Lauri followed me on Twitter. And so I used it as an opportunity to say hi and that I'd actually quoted her in my recent academic masters and that I would be quoting some of her work in my new book, and so we began a conversation. She was, "Oh, I don't really know anything about the Irish police force or what they do," and the conversations developed.

Joanne: Then I suggested to her that she might be a really good person to write the foreword for my book. I know lots of crime journalists because of my work in policing and PR. But I didn't know a crime journalist that understood social media, and I didn't really know a police officer that knew social media enough to write the foreword. They would need a real global view. So she was ideal. She agreed to write the foreword of the book.

Joanne: I also broadcast her into my book launch then, and I interviewed her for a chapter of the book, and then she invited me to speak at her policing conference in Phoenix, Arizona, where I brought 33 copies of my book, because that's all I could carry with the weight in my bag. I sold them all. I could have sold more. I got to speak there, so I spoke to 150 chiefs of police from across the United States and Canada, and included there were the Pentagon. They bought three copies of my book, asked me for some social media advice, and then another person came up to me and said, "Your book is now mandatory reading in the Royal Canadian Mounted Police in Edmonton." And I was like, wow, this is amazing.

Joanne: So that was kind of like my best story all from a tweet, building that relationship. Because we know that the Twitter Graph brings people together through their interests, whereas on Facebook, it's about relationships. So that's kind of been remarkable for me. And then it drove a lot of my book sales, and other speaking opportunities. The other thing that I would say is that even my work with the EU Parliament and the other public sector agencies, that book and that foreword from Lauri really gives me a step in the door. You know, because I have authority. Twitter's been a good friend to me.

PART IV

SOCIAL MEDIA FOR IMPROVING TRAVEL

INTRODUCTION AND MY EXPERIENCES

I 've entitled this set of interviews as Social Travel, even though the two interviews I picked aren't particularly indicative of what is possible. They do fit the category of "Any times when you have gone to a new location and had fun by meeting contacts that you have only previously met on Social Media," but they don't explicitly talk about what is possible travel-wise. Thankfully I do have a lot of personal experience about the power of social media in improving your travel experience.

In my case, like in so many of these situations I found this out by accident rather than explicitly planning things, though I am getting better at the planning element of travel from a social media point of view.

Earlier this year (2018), I went on a prolonged trip to the United States, which I christened my SWAN tour. Purely by accident I had managed to plan a trip to San Diego for Social Media Marketing World(SMMW), then Wichita, then Austin for the South By Southwest conference(SXSW) and finally to New York and then home. Once I realised the first letters of my destinations spelled SWAN, the SWAN tour was christened.

If I'm going to the U.S, due to the fact I'm based in the U.K, I like to make the most of it and I had already booked tickets for SMMW and SXSW, but there was a four day gap between when the weekend after SMMW ended and the start of SXSW. I originally considered just getting to Austin early, but as SXSW is quite long I didn't want to stay for any longer there.

So why go to Wichita? Well, it all stretches back to the fact that I was a regular viewer and commenter on Jen Cole's regular Facebook Live shows.

When Facebook Live was a new thing early in 2017, lots of people I knew were launching regular shows on Facebook, and I tried to support as many of them as I could, to help them through the part where no one was commenting on their shows.

Most people I knew doing these shows gave up, but Jen just kept going, doing two shows a week, one with marketers on Wednesdays and one on Fridays with a variety of local Wichita business people, from musicians, event organisers to the guy who runs a business that sharpens knives. Rather strangely I've got to prefer the Friday shows to the Wednesday show as they gave an interesting glimpse into life in Wichita. Julie Riley became part of the show as she and Jen eventually merged their companies. Jen's friend Stephanie Hartung was also a co-host of the show for a while.

So when it came as a decision as to where to go between SMMW and SXSW it suddenly occurred to me, why don't I visit Wichita? So I booked my trip. I already knew Jen, Julie and Stephanie from hosting the show and I also knew a lot of people less well who had been guests or were regular watchers of the show.

When I eventually got to Wichita because of all the people I already knew I had a really good time, despite never having ever visited the city before at all. They even started using a hashtag #timdayict to document what happened (Jen for some reason thought I was only there for one day rather than three, hence the "day" part of the hashtag).

If I contrast that with SXSW where I hadn't made any connections there beforehand, the difference was palpable. SXSW is an enormous event and it's very easy to get lost in it.

Learning my lesson I went onto Facebook and found as many people as I knew in New York and arranged a meetup one night. This included Christine Gritmon who'd I heard great things about from Jen and Julie while I was in Wichita who somehow I hadn't really met at SMMW.

So that's my story of social travel. The two other examples of this section are of the power of meeting people who you've only previously met on social media. It's exactly the same principle whether done locally or in a different location.

I feel that social media is a bit like air-power, to use a military analogy: it's fantastic in what it can do but you will need to put boots on the ground eventually. In this case, those boots on the ground are meeting people in the real world.

I met Cathy Wassell first online in Twitter chats and then at the MarketEd.Live conference in Derby. Chrissie Parker I have met through the Alliance of Independent Authors.

17

CATHY WASSELL

C athy Wassell is a Facebook Ads and Social Media Strategist at www.sociallycontented.com.

SHE IS SURGICALLY CONNECTED to the internet and delights in finding Facebook Ad targeting that works for even the most niche client.

. . .

Tɪᴍ Lᴇᴡɪs: Any time when you've gone to a new location, and had fun by meeting contacts you've only previously met on social media?

Cathy Wassell: Yes. I'm in a private Facebook group. It's all women. You'll figure out why I am in it: because we wanted to get pregnant, and we joined it, I can't remember what it was called now. It was a group on Facebook for women, who are trying to start families. It was mostly American, but there were people from all over the world. Gradually the real cows became apparent. We set up our own little private, secret Facebook group. My son is nearly 16. I have known them for 17 years. Last year I met them. I had met some before, but last year I met quite a lot of them for the first time.

Cathy Wassell: Unfortunately it wasn't a very nice occasion. I went to America, because one of them had terminal cancer. We all went. We all went to see her basically. But it was still a happy occasion, because we were all seeing each other. She's since died. We don't talk quite so much now, but for a long time, for many years we talked to each other every day. We knew loads about each other.

18

CHRISSIE PARKER

C hrissie lives in Devon, UK, with her husband. She has published six books including Integrate and Temperance (books one and two of The Moon Series), Among the Olive Groves, Nabataea and The Secrets, a collection of Poems and Short Stories.

Wind Across the Nile is her sixth book. Other work includes articles for the Bristolian, The Huffington Post and The Artist

Unleashed. Chrissie also writes regularly for The Zakynthos Informer.

Chrissie's poem Maisie was performed at the 100 poems by 100 women event at the Bath International Literary Festival in 2013. In 2016 Among the Olive Groves won an historical fiction award in the Summer Indie Book Awards.

Chrissie is passionate about Ancient History, Archaeology and Travel, and has completed two Egyptology courses and an Archaeological Techniques course with Exeter University.

To find out more about Chrissie visit her website: www.chrissieparker.com

CHRISSIE PARKER: There is a group called the Exeter Authors Association and last week my South West group kind of slightly pipped them to the post when they were trying to think about organising something, so they called it something slightly different. But there's no animosity: we work together and they're actually lovely people.

Chrissie Parker: I've come across most of them on Twitter, through a Monday night Twitter thing that happens about books, through the Devon Book Club. I've met a number of them through a couple of Facebook Groups. Some of them I've met through the Alliance of Independent Authors Facebook Group. Others I've met through the South West Facebook Group.

Chrissie Parker: They were hosting a pop up bookshop last week in my town, and I was temping. So on the lunchtime I thought, "Do you know what? I'm gonna pop in and just say hello." It was the best lunch hour I'd ever had. Because I walk in and one of them looked at me and she recognised me from my bonkers hat actually, first. And she went "Oh my God! Chrissie!" she ran over and she threw her arms around me and gave me a really big hug. I was just like, "Aww, that's so lovely."

Chrissie Parker: I realised who it was. I was like, "Hi. How are you?" She was like, "Oh my God. Thank you so much for coming in." Then I turned round and there was another one, and another one, and another one. We just spent the nicest 45 minutes chatting books. Chatting everything author. And then we came up with, "Oh. Should we do this next summer? Why don't we have an event between the two of us and just do this huge event and invite everybody, and have a picnic in the park or something like that?" And yeah, it was only 45 minutes but it was really, really nice having met all these people, and had interactions with them on Twitter and on Facebook, to kind of just go in and meet them in the flesh and talk to them.

Chrissie Parker: It was really nice because it wasn't: "Oh now you're here, buy my book." It wasn't anything like that. It was just: "It's so nice to see you. It's so nice to finally meet you, and how are you? And what are you up to?" And me saying: "Oh how's the pop up book-shop going this week and this is a really great idea." Then we just, like I tend to do, tangented about all sorts of things. It was just a really, really lovely experience. It was nice to know that you can meet people on social media and then you can meet them in the flesh, and not only are they just as nice as they are on social media, but actually sometimes they're nicer. And you just think, "Yeah. I'm so glad that I made that connection with these people, because they're just really really lovely and I totally get them and they totally get me and yes, these are people that I can be, certainly acquaintances with, but actually, probably friends with as well."

PART V

OTHER POSITIVE USES OF SOCIAL MEDIA

INTRODUCTION

In this section I include interviews from people who have used social media to improve the world but don't fit into other categories. Clare Josa was part of the EU VAT Campaign that managed to get the European Union to change their new tax rules which were adversely affecting small businesses that sold online products. It's actually through this campaign that I got to know Clare Josa and I met her in person for the first time at the Soulful PR Conference in 2017.

Kim Go is someone I met online and actually met in San Diego after this year's Social Media Marketing World. I found her story of the support group she runs for widowed people touching, and wish I'd known about it when I was widowed.

19

KIM GO

K im Go is an interfaith Minister, former minister of Congregational Life, a public speaker, coach, author, ritual celebrant and expressive facilitator.

Her study-guide for the book Entering the Healing Ground by Francis Weller is currently being used internationally, including in "Healing Circles for Grief and Loss" via Commonweal and she has published articles, an interview and a book chapter with Open to

Hope, a non-profit organisation with the mission of helping people find hope after loss.

She have taken post-graduate studies through the American Art Therapy Association. She has also trained at the Zen Hospice Center in San Francisco, California.

She graduated with a Bachelor's degree in Theater Arts and Music, and a Master's degree in Theology (M.Div). You can find out more about her grief support group at:

http://www.aliveandmortal.org/

KIM GO: I'm trying to think what will be appropriate without giving away confidentiality. But I do believe I have one person that I could speak of and she knows that I talk about these kind of things so I don't think she would have a problem with me mentioning any of this. So she was 38 at the time, her husband, I think, about the same age and he got pneumonia and was in the hospital for I think about four months and then passed away. She had a two year old and a four year old. She ended up in the Facebook group, through I think just searching. A lot of times people in the groups know people and they'll recommend them to come in if they've had a loss or whatever. And she's had numerous problems with deciding how to raise her children.

Kim Go: The other thing that can happen a lot is that people, especially with the economy being stressed, can actually lose their jobs when they're grieving. We had quite a few people that this happened to and she was one. So we were basically her main support base. She's in the other groups, but she says ours is the one that she will come to every week and read what other people are posting and post herself and things like that.

Kim Go: So we have seen her through. She is now gainfully employed again. She has had some discipline issues with her children and they seem to be evening out but she has rested and relied on the wisdom of the group and there are many voices with many opinions. The only thing that's unifying us is the grief. You know, we have really diverse political opinions and really diverse life opinions. So she's rested on the wisdom of all of those people and her life is far more stabilised than it was seven years ago.

Kim Go: We've also had, and this is the tricky thing about social media, people that have been somewhat suicidal in the groups. So I have put up a pinned status post in the group on what we do when someone is suicidal and does decide to post in the group. I have seen several people who were periodically highly suicidal earlier on whose posts are now far more balanced and happy and actually they come in and celebrate positive things that have been happening in their lives. So it seems to not just be the place to go when you're hurting or feeling despair, but also people come back and report their successes and things that are going well and then they support other people.

20

CLARE JOSA

C lare Josa mentors women who want to change the world. As the author of Dare to Dream Bigger, she specialises in setting you free from those secret 3am fears, so you can step up to make the difference you are really here to make in the world - loving the journey. You can find out about Clare at http://www.clarejosa.com/

. . .

CLARE JOSA : So Tim, I really wanted to share with your readers how we used social media to change European law. We're a group of micro-business owners, that means a turnover below two million euros, quite a long way below that for most of us.

Clare Josa : In December 2014 we suddenly heard about a new piece of EU VAT law that had been voted in by the British Government and all the member states to mean that when you sell stuff digitally, the place of supply is no longer where the business was, but where the consumer was.

Clare Josa : Which makes sense because VAT is a sales tax: it should be done based on the place of supply. The problem was that we don't have access to the data to prove to audit standards where the customer was. So we were left with the choice of breaking the law or closing our businesses.

Clare Josa : A group of us were in somebody else's Facebook group and just said "Where's the campaign group? How can we support them?" Oh, there isn't one, here's the campaign group, who would like to support us? Not one of us had ever met the others before. We formed our tiny, little secret Facebook group; we were involved in somebody else's group talking about digital bank, quickly realised that group was actually a really negative place to be.

Clare Josa : So we needed to set up somewhere more positive, and within a few weeks we had our first meeting with the UK Government, with the man that runs the UK tax authority and with the minister responsible for the rules. And at that point it was the first time anybody had ever told them during the consultation process that there was going to be a problem, and we have two weeks to change the law. Which is obviously not gonna happen. But social media brought us together.

Clare Josa : Without that group of women, we wouldn't have got that meeting. By the end of the campaign, it's actually being voted on, on December the 5th at the Ecofin meeting* with the finance minsters from all the member states for the thresholds that our data proved we needed. So we're really hoping that's going get passed next week. But where social media helped us was galvanising the campaigners.

Clare Josa : We ended up with a group of a couple of thousand businesses just in the one Facebook group. Across the EU, I led a piece a quantitative research that was actually used by the European Commission to justify the threshold. So Deloitte got paid a million somethings to do their own research that didn't get published, and ours did for free. But that couldn't happen without social media. We would organise campaigns where people wrote to their MEPs and that's been shown to be pivotal in getting some of the states that were objecting to this threshold, to agree to it. We've had people writing to their finance ministers, we've had them visiting their MPs, their MEPs and the thing that really kicked off the campaign was a Twitter storm.

Clare Josa : We managed to get the hashtag #EUVAT trending on Twitter, worldwide. And it was that Twitter storm that got the press's attention, that meant that the UK tax authority and Government stopped ignoring us and it got us the attention of the EU Commission. It started the journey for me to be invited to the European Parliament to give keynote speeches to MEPs and key lobbyists and decision makers.

Clare Josa : It got us consultative status with HMRC and with the European Commission. All because of social media, and without social media, if all we'd had was a mailing list, we wouldn't have been able to galvanise the positive emotion. That's what social media did for us. So mailing list is you talking to one person at a time. Social media brings them together and creates a community or tribe and without that tribe, we would not have achieved what we achieved. When people keep saying the gold is in the email list, yes they're right. But the community is in social media.

* NOTE THAT THE ECOFIN MEETING VOTED TO IMPLE-MENT THE CHANGES AFTER THIS INTERVIEW TOOK PLACE.

HOW TO SOCIAL NETWORK

1

WHAT HAVE I LEARNED FROM THE INTERVIEWS?

I have learned a lot in the course of interviewing people for this book. In some ways it has confirmed a view that I have been developing for some time: the rather obvious idea that you need to be social on social media.

I am sure some of you will be saying "what does that mean?" Let me explain. There are three main aspects of social media: creating content, consuming content and interacting with content. When I refer to content, I'm talking about the things people post, put on their profile, publish or put out in their stories.

TOO MANY PEOPLE just focus on the first of these. So they set up automated programs to tweet out links to all their old blog articles, or automated programs to post out direct links to sales pages. Automation isn't bad, and I do think that people should do a certain amount of this, but doing this alone misses out a great deal of the real power of social media, which is where the social media networking side really comes in.

Consuming other people's content is often seen as time-wasting and while indeed this can be true, I think this can apply to creating content as well. I think you do need to be careful what posts you read and watch, but don't underestimate the pleasure the creators of content get out of people consuming and interacting with their posts.

I SEPARATE out consuming from interacting with posts, as lots of people (myself included at times) share and like posts that they clearly haven't read or watched, mainly because they like the person or are returning the favour of the person sharing their content. I'd hasten a guess that the majority of content shared on social media hasn't been fully read or consumed by the people sharing it.

THIS IS a large chunk of the reason fake news and urban myths spread so quickly. Most people read the headline and look at who shared the post and that determines whether they will "like" the post. While people also comment on posts they haven't properly consumed, this is less likely.

IF YOU LOOK at the interviews in this book, almost all cases involve people doing some combination of all three of these activities.

Given the noise on social media, being found in search on most networks is getting progressively harder, and having people seeing the content you produce is again a lot harder than it was previously. So consuming content and interacting with it is becoming much more important.

IT HAS BECOME a little bit of a cliché to say "be human" on social media, but it is very true, at least when it comes to networking. I have been unable to find people who are following a step-by-step formula to get their opportunities.

. . .

I'VE BEEN at a conference where someone has appeared from nowhere and the conversation has gone something like this:

> *Random Person: "Hi I am X."*
> *Tim: "Hi, I am Tim."*
> *Random Person: "I sell multi-variant widget coding*
>   *solutions, what do you do?"*
> *Tim: "Oh I podcast about self-publishing and write books."*
> *Random Person: "Here's my business card. Great to*
>   *meet you."*
> *Tim: "Oh here's mine."*

At which point Mr Random walks off to the next person and does the same thing. Then after the conference I get an e-mail from Mr Random, or sometimes even something in the post. But I have no connection with the guy, and unless I really want a multi-variant widget coding solution (which isn't actually a thing by the way!) then the most I'll do is add him as a connection on LinkedIn.

TOO OFTEN PEOPLE are trying to do the same thing on social media. I am not saying that you can't have some success doing this kind of thing if you scale it up enough, but just that you are going to be up against lots of other people doing the same thing with progressively diminishing returns. On social media, this almost invariably requires quite a large amount of coding and a constant war with the social media networks themselves as they stop people from doing what they consider spammy things.

BUT CLEARLY "BE SOCIAL" and "be human" is too general advice. So in the next section I'll give some more specific advice on how to actually do social media networking.

2

HOW DO YOU DO SOCIAL MEDIA NETWORKING

Y ou will often hear that "it's not what you know but who you know" that matters and as I've got older I certainly think that is true.

But I'd guess many of you are crying "But I don't know anyone!" and getting ready to throw this book into the bin.

BUT PLEASE DON'T as it is surprisingly easy to get to know relevant people as long as you are willing to be patient and flexible.

GETTING yourself setup

THE FIRST THING TO do is to get yourself established on the social media platforms. I always recommend people start with Twitter. This may seem odd as Facebook is the larger network, but there are a number of reasons for this:

- Twitter is really very open. You can find people, follow anyone, reply to anyone and see all of their conversations.
- It is easy to "fake" looking important on Twitter. There is a follow-back culture. I know people will hate me for saying this, but I'd say 90% of accounts with huge numbers of followers aren't particularly important people. But there is still a residual amount of respect you get for your Twitter following.
- Twitter chats are a fantastic place to find like-minded people and to get the more important deep connections.
- People are less surprised when someone they don't know gets involved in their conversations on Twitter, as opposed to the other platforms.

So SET up a Twitter account (if you don't have one already) and make sure you set up a photo, have a sensible profile description and ideally a nice looking Twitter header photo.

A GREAT FREE site for creating graphics for social media is canva.com (select "Twitter header" from their templates for the Twitter header).

ONCE YOU HAVE A TWITTER ACCOUNT, I would recommend using a policy of following relevant people to build up the number of followers on your account to a reasonable level (up to about a thousand or so). I have talked about how to do this on my blog here:

http://stonehampress.com/blog/building_up_a_twitter_following_fast/

I'D ALSO RECOMMEND SETTING up a Facebook personal profile (in the very unlikely situation you don't have one), an Instagram personal profile and a LinkedIn personal profile. These are the best platforms for networking in my opinion. It makes sense to use the same handle on Twitter and Instagram, if possible.

Who to look **for**

After you have set up all your profiles, you need to start looking to connect with the kind of people you are interested in getting to know, which varies by your objective:

- For finding a job then you want to be looking to connect with people in the industry and relevant journalists.
- For looking for romance, find people interested in topics that you are passionate about and look to find communities where you can interact with other people interested in those topics, preferably containing a large proportion of the kind of people you are interested in.
- For making connections for arranging speaking gigs, you want to be looking for conference organisers, speakers at conferences and people related to the topics that you want to be talking about.
- For travel or location-related objectives you want to be looking to make connections and groups related to the area you are interested in going to.

As hopefully has been clear from the interviews, it is much better to look for a category of people rather than obsessing too much about individuals.

·   ·   ·

ADDITIONALLY, it's often equally important to look for groups of people, which can be in:

- Twitter chats
- General discussions around a hashtag on Twitter/Instagram. This is especially true for conferences and events.
- Facebook Groups
- Audiences watching Facebook Live and Periscope broadcasts
- LinkedIn Groups (these have fallen out of favour at time of writing, but LinkedIn are making efforts to revive them).

AS WITH ANY kind of communication, it's a lot harder to make connections if you are trying to rush from not knowing someone to being their best friend. Ideally you want to be moving slowly getting to know people. Being in the same online community as someone helps people get to know you, as people will observe your interactions with other people, as well as your interactions with them directly, helping to accelerate this process.

IN THE NEXT section we talk about how to find people and groups to follow and connect with.

3

FINDING PEOPLE AND GROUPS

S o how do you find these people and groups? This is where search on the social networks is your friend, especially on Twitter and LinkedIn.

TWITTER HAS AN ADVANCED SEARCH FUNCTION, which they seem to go out of their way to hide, which is really powerful. You can read about it here. At the time of writing, you either need to just search for something and then select "advanced search" from the "Search Filters" or bookmark the advanced search page and go there directly.

IT WILL SEARCH Twitter returning both tweets and accounts that are potentially relevant to the search. To begin with, the normal search on Twitter may be enough, but on advanced search you can add a location and a time and date range: this can make your search so much more relevant.

GIVE some thought as to what you are going to search for, refining your search if necessary. For example if you are interested in looking for a job as an accountant in New York, then you could search for "accountant" and set the location as "New York".

Try searches until the results look like the kind you are looking for. Then you should do the following:

- Click the People tab and then follow the accounts shown and add them to a Twitter List. Be aware if you create a public Twitter List then the people added to the list will see they have been added, so give it an impressive title like "New York Accountancy Experts" rather than "random New York Accountants".
- Scan the tweets and look for references to the same hashtag over and over again: these may be commonly used industry hashtags, or those used in a Twitter chat. Also look for handles of people mentioned. These may be people who are important in the industry ("influencers"). You want to follow them and add them to your list (and possibly another list as well).

Unlike LinkedIn and Facebook, you can follow people and see their content without them having to confirm the friendship. You can potentially use a similar approach on Instagram, though there is less opportunity for interaction there generally.

LinkedIn Search is also extremely powerful and is worth using. Though more for research than as a way to build up connections. Similar to advanced Twitter Search, you can specify lots of extra things.

You need to click on "All Filters" on a search, and then you can do things like specify individual companies.

· · ·

So for example if you want to find a list of people who work for Google in Denver you can search for this on LinkedIn's people search.

In LinkedIn, unlike on Facebook, you can attach a message to a connection request. If you have set up your LinkedIn profile to make it appealing, it is possible you could risk attempting to make the connection to the person from this search if you approach with a decent reason for connecting. The lower risk approach is to see if this person is on Twitter and follow them there.

LinkedIn search is amazing for finding out who works at particular organisations and what position they have.

You can search groups on LinkedIn, but currently the search options are by name only. However, by joining relevant groups it does give you a way to find people to connect with on LinkedIn. Some groups are related to events or are closed, so if you don't get accepted by a group then don't worry.

Similarly search on Facebook can be used to find Facebook groups to follow. You want to set the option for "Public Groups" in the search though.

You can also use Google to find things like the hashtags used for Twitter chats by typing "Twitter chat" followed by the topic you are looking for, or look in Twitter chat directories like www.tweetreports.com

· · ·

HOPEFULLY A SELECTION of searches on these platforms should help to provide a list of accounts and groups to monitor. The next stage is learning how to monitor and interact with people on social media which I will cover in the next section.

4

HOW TO MONITOR AND INTERACT ON SOCIAL MEDIA

A valid question with the interviews was how intentional people were in their efforts to connect on social media. Is it just a case that these people were just lucky? Did I pick 20 lucky people out of thousands of people who fail to get anything out of social media? Is it all luck? Honestly I'd say no. In most cases, the reason is that these were people who were willing to put the time and effort to interact with other people on social media, to build relationships rather than using some kind of formula to look for success.

BUT HOW DO you manage your time and efforts on social media on a day-to-day basis in the efforts to reach your objectives? That is what I am going to attempt to cover in this section.

Hopefully now you should have set up a series of Twitter lists with relevant people you are following, and be a member of several Facebook and maybe LinkedIn groups around relevant topic areas. Maybe you have found one or more relevant Twitter chats to participate in. How do you keep in touch with what is happening but not let social media take over your life?

. . .

THE FIRST ISSUE is ensuring your phone is set up correctly. You want to be able to work without your phone constantly interrupting you because someone has commented on your post on social media or sent you a message. All the social media apps let you configure both when you get notifications and what happens on your phone app when these occur. I would suggest that you carefully configure these. You don't want to have a phone notification (e.g a message or a beep) appear when anything happens on social media. Instead let the applications show you with a number of queued notifications against the badge icon of the app, so you know there are notifications waiting, but they don't interrupt you when they occur. Also ensure you don't get e-mails for notifications from these social networks.

SO NOW YOU'VE stopped the social media phone apps from sending you notifications, you want to set up your own custom notifications! This might sound odd, but you do need to be reminded to do things on social media, just you don't want social media to drive what those things are.

ON YOUR PHONE you want to set up notifications on the Reminders app if you use an iPhone or something like Any.do on an Android phone to set up daily reminders to tell you to do things. These should be things like monitoring those Twitter lists (do one for each list), any relevant hashtags (e.g #journorequest) and checking groups that you have joined. This will encourage you to give priority to these things. You should vary how often, and what, you create notifications on, based on the amount of time you have at particular times of day and what seems to be most efficient.

THE SECOND ISSUE TO avoid is getting side-tracked on social media when you get onto it. I struggle with this, as I think everyone does. If you use apps like Tweetdeck on a computer, or Echofon on a phone you can set them up to just view your Twitter lists, or a particular hashtag. For Facebook and LinkedIn, on a computer you can set up shortcuts to particular Facebook Groups and LinkedIn Groups, so you don't need to look at your main newsfeed unless you want to.

So this covers how to set yourself up to monitor these potential connections; how do you actually interact on social media? You should begin by consuming content from relevant people and groups. You will learn a lot. If you are looking for a job, you will learn which companies are most active on social media, who the most active people at those companies are and which people and companies have the best reputation.

IF YOU ARE LOOKING for romance you can observe the balance of men and women and get some time to judge the character of people. In some cases it will also be obvious which people are in relationships. If you are looking for opportunities then you can learn a lot about where and when the conferences are and who is speaking at which event. If you are looking to go to a new location and find people to connect with then you start to learn who and what is important in that area.

BUT YOU DO at some stage need to go beyond just consuming relevant content. You need to start interacting and eventually producing your own posts. Interaction can start fairly painlessly almost immediately by "liking" relevant posts on Facebook, LinkedIn and Twitter and later retweeting and sharing posts. You do need to be careful to make sure you don't unintentionally like or share anything that is potentially offensive or something you don't agree with. You can after a while judge by the source how much effort you need to give to reading a post before liking it. In an ideal world you'd read and watch all of every post you consume on social media, but usually time constraints make this not possible. It's generally wise to shy away from political or religious topics, unless of course this relates to the people you are trying to connect with.

THE MOST IMPORTANT kind of interaction is of course commenting on people's posts, either as tweet replies, or as comments on Facebook and LinkedIn. This can be intimidating at first, especially if the people who are posting are industry leaders or, in the romantic sense especially, someone you really like, but the benefits of commenting are so much more than just clicking like or retweet.

SO WHAT DO you comment on? A simple "good post" or replying to a question only gets you so far. I would suggest the following:

- Provide useful relevant information, for example extra information the poster missed out or didn't know about.
- Ask a question that asks for clarification or more information on something that wasn't clear in the original post.
- Provide humour, though be careful with people you haven't interacted with much.
- Provide backing for the poster's opinion.
- Introducing them to someone else who might be helpful, and is related to the post in question.
- Respectfully provide a counter-argument to the poster's opinion.

Make sure you know and adhere to any group rules in Facebook or LinkedIn groups. Never demean or be rude to the commenter, even if you disagree strongly with their opinion. Always try to maintain the attitude that "you wish them well". Some groups and social network users can be very hard to deal with. You will have people who never get your jokes, or deliberately misunderstand what you write. With cases of genuine abuse, please report the people to the social network or group manager.

THE IDEAL IS that your comment will evoke a response from the original poster, or from other users and you can get a conversation going. You will gradually start to form relationships with people once this happens a few times. On a network like Twitter, you can almost immediately follow people you have interacted with and in many cases you will get a follow-back. On Facebook and LinkedIn it can take longer to get to the point where a friend or connection request is appropriate. But having a decent conversation in the comments on a post is a great way to tilt the odds that they will accept a connection request.

YOU HAVE TO NOTE THAT, of course, the amount of interaction with a person before they will consider you worthy of connecting with will vary from person to person and from network to network. Generally Twitter requires the least effort and Facebook the most. On Twitter, if someone is following relatively few people compared to who is following them, then that is a sign that they aren't going to be able to be that easy to connect with. But even in this case, it doesn't mean that person isn't worth interacting with, as being officially connected with someone is only a small part of the networking process.

A MORE IMPORTANT aim is being able to get to the situation where you can send someone a direct message on social media and start a private exchange. This is actually where watching content like people's Instagram and Facebook stories can be worthwhile, as they allow you to send people messages referring to whatever was in that particular part of the story. So if you see someone's story about them visiting Barcelona, you can message them and mention how much you liked the Sagrada Familia or something like that.

. . .

ANOTHER FANTASTIC OPPORTUNITY is to watch people's live broadcasts (on Facebook, Periscope or Instagram) and comment while the broadcast is going on. For those people who do respond to comments it can be a great way to make a connection with them. Most people struggle to get that much interaction to their live broadcasts, so will really appreciate intelligent or amusing comments. For broadcasts by people or organisations with a large following, the value comes in the interactions with other people watching the same broadcast. This is especially true for regularly scheduled content where the same people tend to turn up for every show.

NONE OF NETWORKING is rocket science; generally the principles are to show interest, attention and care. If you aren't interested in what someone is posting then however suitable they may be as a prospect for networking, then you probably should focus on other people. We all know there are people who are good at faking this, but even if we overlook this isn't a nice thing to do, there are usually so many people out there that you are better off giving your attention to those people who you do like and enjoy their content.

WE HAVE NOW MENTIONED CONSUMING content, and talking about interactions, and in the next section we talk about creating content.

5

WHAT CONTENT SHOULD YOU CREATE?

Given that content marketing is very much in vogue at the moment, it may surprise you that I'm not going to recommend that people interested in social media networking start doing any kind of large-scale content creation immediately.

By large-scale content creation I am referring to creating a blog (written information on a website), a podcast (a regular audio show) or video show (for example a YouTube show or as a regular live show on Facebook).

There are many good reasons for creating regular content and either posting links to it or, in the case of live shows, actually doing it on social media, but from a pure connectivity point of view I'm not sure they are worth the time, at least at the beginning.

I AM SAYING this as the host of a podcast (Begin Self-Publishing) with over 130 episodes done over several years. Having a podcast has certainly helped in terms of making your existing connections deeper (mainly by interviewing people), but I do feel from a purely networking point of view the time might have been spent better elsewhere. Running a podcast or a blog requires a lot of time, and if your focus is not building an audience (for personal fame, hobby interest or to sell to them), but rather to connect with people then you should seriously consider if it is the right thing to do.

You should certainly be creating content in terms of posting interesting or amusing short-form content on these social media, as much to show people your accounts are active. You can schedule out posts on these platforms, either on the platforms themselves or by using software like Buffer or Agorapulse. One advantage of larger-scale content is that it makes it easier to find things to post, but most social media platforms show posts with links in them to less people than just normal text or video posts.

So what kind of thing should you post:

- Posts to demonstrate knowledge on a topic.
- Provide useful information to the community you are trying to reach.
- Ask a question. This can be to provoke an answer or to genuinely find out the answer to something you want to know.
- Provide humour, though be very careful as this could get shared anywhere.
- Recommending a resource (someone else's blog or podcast, for example) while tagging that person. Do this for something you genuinely like, not just because you want to get in with a particular person.
- An update as to what is happening in your life: this is especially true for posts to an Instagram or Facebook story.
- What you see if you are at a conference or some kind of event with a hashtag.
- Links to where you have been interviewed on other people's shows or mentioned on their blogs.

I THINK if your aim is to find a job then I think any content you produce should show your knowledge and interest in the kind of job you are looking for. If you are looking for romance then you should probably be concentrating on showing intelligence and humour in those groups you join. In both those cases I believe you may have to try and subtly make it known that you are available for employment opportunities or romance. I have seen people flat out state they are looking for a job or romance on social media, but I'm not sure how successful this approach is. It's certainly something you can clearly mention if you are made redundant or leave a relationship, but more generally it probably has to be mentioned more subtly. Also if you get clients from social media then this of course allows a more open approach.

IN TERMS of other uses of social media networking I think you can be much more forward in what you are looking for, as they aren't so exclusive: if you do one speaking event it doesn't mean you are espousing all other speaking events. That said, whatever the situation you shouldn't always be posting asking about your final objective. You will get a reputation on social media, and you really want that to be mainly because you are providing value or entertainment to people and not because you clearly want something.